LED ZEPPELIN REVEALED

Publisher and Creative Director: Nick Wells
Project Editor: Polly Willis
Designer: Theresa Maynard
Production: Chris Herbert and Claire Walker
Special thanks to Chelsea Edwards, Geoffrey Meadon and Julia Rolf

First Published 2008 by
FLAME TREE PUBLISHING
Crabtree Hall
Crabtree Lane
Fulham
London SW6 6TY

www.flametreepublishing.com

Copyright © Flame Tree Publishing Limited

13 15 17 16 14
5 7 9 10 8 6 4

A copy of the CIP data for this book is available from the British Library.

ISBN: 978-1-84451-733-6
Special ISBN: 978-0-6815-4440-6

Picture Credits
Corbis: Barnabas Bosshart: 65

Foundry Arts: 21 (b), 31 (bl, br), 46, 52 (b), 60, 63 (t), 78, 89 (b), 92, 102 (r), 114, 127 (tl), 128 (b), 141 (t), 155 (bl), 156 (bl, br), 159 (bl), 163 (l), 165 (bl), 167 (tr), 168 (tr), 170 (bl), 173 (b), 175 (t), 177 (bl, br), 179 (bl), 181 (bl), 185 (t, b), 186 (br), 188 (bl, br), 193 (bl), 196 (l)

Getty Images: Charles Bonnay: 28, 43 (t), 45, 64, 157, 177; Lester Cohen: 191; Ian Cook: 171; DMI: 163; Jo Hale: 195; Hulton Archive: 18, 86, 107, 127, 144, 155, 176, 190; Anwar Hussein: 194; Walter Iooss Jr.: 87, 88; Jeffrey Mayer: 104; Kevin Mazur: 187; Michael Ochs Archive: 25, 44, 54, 62, 72, 100, 101, 110, 126, 129, 151, 154, 172, 183; Paul Natkin: 168; Laurance Ratner: 108 (tl), 121; Bob Strong: 181; Marty Temme: 170, 173; Chris Walter: 52, 56; Kevin Westenberg: 196; Louise Wilson: 193

Redferns: Richard E. Aaron: 94, 128, 134, 138, 156; Cyrus Andrews: 14, 30; Jorgen Angel: 31, 36, 38, 48, 67, 70, 81, 93, 97, 106; RB: 12, 26; Dick Barnatt: 39; Carey Brandon: 186; Charlie Gillett Archive: 37; Fin Costello: 84, 178; Grant Davis: 169; Phil Dent: 166; George Desota: 136; Ian Dickson: 116, 118, 119, 130, 140; EMI Archives: 13, 15; Fotex Agentur GMBH: 149; GAB Archives: 41, 43 (b), 61, 102 (l), 103, 112, 139, 160, 183 (inset); Harry Goodwin: 21; Herb Greene: 59; Ron Howard: 22; Mick Hutson: 180, 185; Ivan Keeman: 24; Bob King: 174; John Lynn Kirk: 113, 122; Robert Knight: 34, 42, 50, 76, 79, 89, 90, 96, 120, 183 (main); Hayley Madden: 192; Gered Mankowitz: 20, 40; Chris Morphet: 35; Ilpo Musto: 159; Peter Pakvis: 179; Ed Perlstein: 132, 135; Jan Persson: 47, 68, 85; David Redfern: 17, 75, 98, 99, 108 (r), 109, 115, 137, 148, 189; Ebet Roberts: 158, 162, 164, 165; Brian Shuel: 16; Chuck Stewart: 71, 184; Peter Still: 150, 188; Gai Terrell: 53; Rob Verhost: 142, 146

TopFoto: 58, 66, 74, 77, 80

JASON DRAPER (author) comes from Plymouth and currently lives in London. He is the Reviews Editor at *Record Collector*, the monthly music magazine dedicated to collecting music of all genres and on all formats. He has written for *Uncut*, *Metal Hammer*, *Sound Nation*, *The Big Issue Cymru* and *Buzz*. He was a contributor to *The Definitive Illustrated Encyclopedia of Rock* and has written *The Rolling Stones Revealed* and *Classic Album Covers* (all Flame Tree Publishing).

PAUL DU NOYER (Introduction) began his career on the *New Musical Express*, went on to edit *Q* and to found *Mojo*. He also helped to launch *Heat* and several music websites. As well as editing several rock reference books, he is the author of *We All Shine On*, about the solo music of John Lennon, and *Wondrous Place*, a history of the Liverpool music scene. He is nowadays an contributing editor of *The Word*.

Printed in China

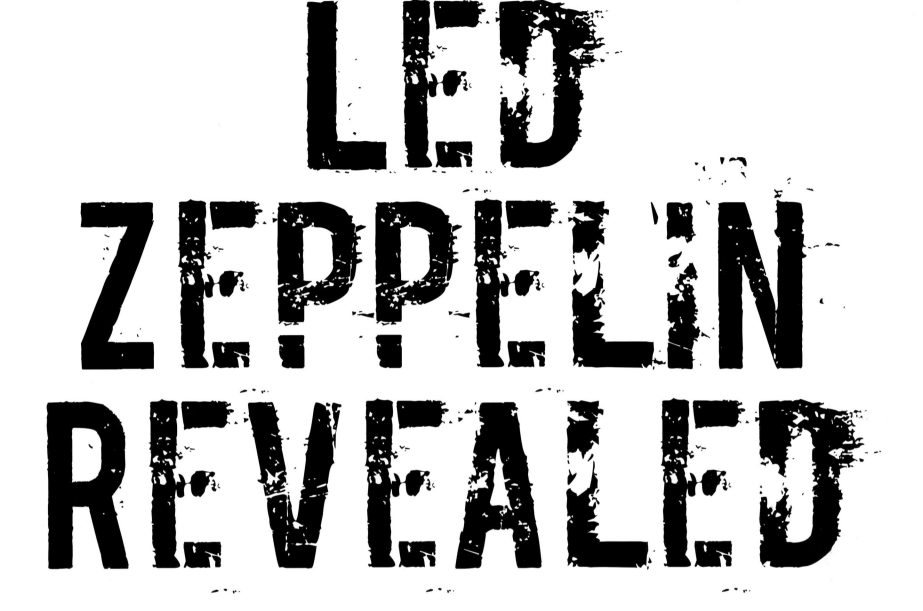

LED ZEPPELIN REVEALED

TEXT BY JASON DRAPER

INTRODUCTION BY PAUL DU NOYER

FLAME TREE
PUBLISHING

CONTENTS

INTRODUCTION

Nobody who has heard Led Zeppelin would ever need their memory jogged. As somebody once said of the band's music: 'Hoary blues motifs were pumped up to enormous proportions, clubbed senseless by Bonham's colossal wallop, panicked to distraction by Page's crazed air-raid riffs, pummelled by Jones's slum-demolishing bass-lines, and strangled by Plant's lascivious shrieks of lust.' And they mentioned, just for good measure: 'thick, churning streams of molten noise and melodic patterns of tortuous intricacy, vocals clawing up the octaves or crawling piteously, low and moaning.'

Descriptions of Led Zeppelin can seem somewhat over-the-top (and I confess the examples above were both my own fault) but what of it? Here was a band who traded in superlatives of every sort. They were the biggest, the best, the worst-behaved, the most contrary, the loudest and yet the most delicate, the most of everything you cared to name. It is impossible to speak of Led Zeppelin without some sense of awe at what they achieved, even if it failed to touch your heart or stir your soul. But then, if Led Zeppelin have never stirred your soul, you're unlikely to be reading this. So let's just assume we're among friends and press on joyfully with a celebration of the greatest hard-rock band of all time.

Led Zeppelin combined power and subtlety better than anyone before or since. They understood drama and they understood dynamics. They were a magical conflation of four exceptional performers who were profoundly different personalities. They took mastery of the recording studio to new levels, but it was the live shows that made them a phenomenon. On stage, John Bonham's drums were described by Jimmy Page as sounding 'like cannons'. Page himself, the musical generalissimo, had only to don the twin-necked Gibson guitar that signalled 'Stairway To Heaven' for entire stadia to erupt. Robert Plant's rock-god limbs would emerge from his skimpy blouse and he grasped the mic like a lover. And in the shadows, the bass of John Paul Jones conspired with Bonham's drumming to forge a rhythm section tighter than anything except their singer's trousers. Light and shade, then. As another description of Led Zeppelin has it: 'Leningrad meets Laura Ashley'.

It's safe to assume their music will live for ever more, but Led Zeppelin left another sort of legacy besides. They left legends. They created a sort of epic adventure tale that still looms large in rock mythology. I don't claim for a moment that all those stories are true, for much of Led Zep's notoriety stemmed from the wishful thinking of young male fans and the requirements of sensationalist publishing. But the rumours arising from their American tours, especially, were an unstoppable force. The band, so we were told, returned after gigs to their fabled lair on Sunset Boulevard's Continental Hyatt House, known thereafter as the 'Riot House'. Installed in all their glory, so the scenario continues, the decadent princelings devoured virgin sacrifices and refined the varied arts of rock'n'roll debauchery – with just an added dash of black magic wickedness.

None of which sits well with the group's surviving members. They play down the lurid side at every opportunity. 'It was California that was naughty, not Led Zeppelin,' said Robert Plant, not entirely convincingly. John Paul Jones asserts he simply wasn't around. And the late John Bonham, who certainly was around

when there was mischief to be made, can no longer explain himself. When I asked Jimmy Page, he was emphatic in dismissing the band's sordid reputation: 'Things did get a bit over the top as far as some of the reported things. But I mean, that's like Peeping Tom, isn't it? It's Peeping Tom but it's worse than that, because it's Peeping Tom fantasising. …'

Whatever the facts, Led Zeppelin always looked fantastical enough to spawn speculation and fire the fans' imaginations. Page and Plant were hippy cavaliers, though decidedly a step on from the generation of peace and love. There was a heaviness about them that chimed with a new mood in the early 1970s, less idealistic than Woodstock and far less innocent than the flower children of the 1960s. But they were glamorous beyond the dreams of any dandruffed heavy metallers – whose genre the group helped invent, yet immediately transcended. They really could look more than mortal. And they carried an urgent, sexual energy. Unlike The Rolling Stones they had no historical baggage (though each

was an experienced player) and were unashamedly a young man's band for the coming era. For all their satin and curls they re-asserted a kind of masculine force in hard rock, whose chosen weapons were volume and phallic posturing. Not for nothing was the new term 'cock rock' coined around this time.

So they were flashy, proudly self-sufficient and apparently without an important social message for their followers. For all these reasons, like their pop counterpart Marc Bolan of T.Rex, Led Zeppelin were not popular with senior critics, who were rooted in the late 1960s counter-culture and pursued the notion of 'selling out' with a puritanical zeal. There was some hostility, too, from commentators with a Women's Lib background, although the concept of sexism would take until the late 1970s to reach the mainstream of rock press and another decade to get beyond that to society at large. There were valid objections, also, to the band's deployment of certain blues material without due acknowledgement to its African-American instigators.

Despite all these misgivings, Led Zeppelin thrived. So mighty had they become by the early 1970s that their huge, fearsome manager Peter Grant could now demand unprecedented percentages from promoters. They overturned the economic models of the rock business even as they were re-inventing its sound and shifting its aesthetic. It's as if, in the sudden absence of The Beatles (who split up in 1970), someone had to take the lead and it happened to be Zeppelin. Fundamentally, they changed the basis of the music business from the single to the album, which was far more lucrative and formed a deeper, more lasting bond with the fans. Resisting any surrender of control, they shunned TV appearances just as they shunned singles in their homeland – an irony, when you consider that 'Whole Lotta Love' became the BBC's *Top Of The Pops*' theme tune.

Many vested interests were rubbed up the wrong way when Led Zeppelin passed through town. It's no wonder the band had such a turbulent ride, nor that they depended upon the forceful bulk of Peter Grant to shield them from the fall-out. The rock writer and movie director Cameron Crowe (of *Almost Famous* fame) recalled seeing Grant introduce himself to Bob Dylan. And Dylan's laconic reply? 'I don't come to you with "my" problems, do I?'

No matter. The crucial thing was that Led Zeppelin understood each other, and on stage that mutual understanding hit telepathic heights. Watch their in-concert DVDs for glimpses of the knowing smiles that shoot across from one player to the next. (And I wonder, incidentally, if Robert Plant invented the air guitar? Note how he tackles the singer's recurrent challenge of looking occupied while your guitarist takes a solo: Plant shimmies up to Page in a display of reverent mimickry.) Between the leonine sexual strut of the frontman, the restless ingenuity of the guitarist and the meticulously synchronized wallop of the rhythm section, their intuitive solidarity could not survive the loss of a single constituent. When John Bonham died in 1980 there was little doubt that everything was over. 'We were above all else an ambient band,' Jimmy Page told me. 'That was the key thing about it.' They were, as all immortal bands must be, a whole much greater than the sum of its parts.

Sure, we describe Led Zeppelin with war-like metaphors: 'bombardment', 'Blitzkrieg' and 'conquest'. And of course they were lustful and pulsating, when lustful and pulsating were required. But as well as their grounding in the blues they had a

brilliant grasp of folk music – they could in fact have chosen that route from the start, had they wished. Every Led Zeppelin fan, at some level, appreciates the intelligent range of this band's music. No wonder that 'Stairway', the madrigal that rises to a maelstrom, remains the emblematic Led Zeppelin song. Their art cannot be contained in glib one-liners.

A Zeppelin devotee in younger days, I had the thrill, in later life, of reuniting Page, Plant and Jones on stage to receive a magazine award. It was their first time in public, in Britain, since the split. I announced them from the stage, uncertain whether they'd even turned up. But as 'Kashmir' boomed majestically from the speakers, they strolled contentedly to the rostrum. 'So many of the songs we did,' said Robert Plant, grinning helplessly, 'we're still very proud of and they still stand up today. They were recorded in the least amount of time and often with the greatest amount of laughter. That's what this award is for, having a ridiculously crazy time.'

THE PRE-LED ZEPPELIN YEARS: 1960-67

1960-67

The supergroup to end all supergroups, Led Zeppelin were often unfairly viewed by the press as a corporate entity that had not paid its dues. You only have to look at the history, however, to see how wrong that is.

It must have been fate. At the same time as Robert Plant (b. 1948) and John Bonham (1948–80) were working the music circuit in the Midlands, playing and getting their experience with various bands before moving up in the ranks of known musicians, over in London two like-minded musicians were doing the same in the local music scene. Jimmy Page (b. 1944) had been playing in front of live crowds since his teens, and John Paul Jones (b. 1946) had been working behind the scenes on various artists' records at the same time. Both quickly made a name for themselves and rose to the upper echelons of session musicians while even releasing their own solo singles. Page became an indispensable session musician and producer for the likes of Decca and Immediate, while Jones would become right-hand session man for Mickie Most.

Before Led Zeppelin was even an entity, between them Page and Jones had played on tracks recorded by ex-Shadows members, The Kinks, The Who, Marianne Faithfull and Tom Jones. But they were far too talented to remain back-room men, and it wouldn't be long before they got their chance to move to the front-line of rock'n'roll's greatest icons.

1960

Jimmy Page: FIRST-EVER SERIOUS 'GIG'

Aged just 16, Jimmy Page – whose first guitar was a steel-stringed Spanish guitar on which he learnt to play skiffle, before quickly moving on to rock'n'roll and the electric guitar – played his first ever serious 'gig'. Though he had been in local bands before, playing for British poet Royston Ellis at London's Mermaid Theatre was his first high-profile performance. Page accompanied the Beatnik-influenced poet on acoustic guitar, having rediscovered a taste for the instrument after listening to British folk star (and future member of Pentangle) Bert Jansch.

1961

Jimmy Page:
WARMS UP FOR CHRIS FARLOWE & THE THUNDERBIRDS

Page would often play in the support band at his local Epsom dance hall and, one night in 1961, he warmed up for Chris Farlowe & The Thunderbirds and Johnny Kidd & The Pirates (above), two early British rock'n'roll acts. Even as a support act, Page's guitar-playing captivated the young audience. London-based singer Neil Christian was one audience member that night and he asked Page to join his band, Neil Christian & The Crusaders.

1962

John Paul Jones: GETS BIG BREAK

Leaving school aged 17, John Paul Jones (then still known by his birth name, John Baldwin) got the first job he auditioned for when he tried out for Jet Harris & Tony Meehan (left), two founder members of British rock'n'roll stalwarts The Shadows. Harris and Meehan had just left their group and recently had a No. 1 hit single with 'Diamonds' (on which, ironically, Jimmy Page had played guitar). Baldwin would play with Harris & Meehan for 18 months and, in 1964, aged 18, changed his name to John Paul Jones and released an instrumental single 'Baja'/'A Foggy Day In Vietnam'.

Jimmy Page: PLAYS WITH THE CRUSADERS

Having been asked to join Neil Christian & The Crusaders in 1961, Page gigged around London with the band, playing covers of American rock'n'roll songs by the likes of Chuck Berry. By far The Crusaders's biggest asset, even at the young age of 17, Page played with the most up-to-date guitar equipment. Allegedly one of the first London guitarists to play with a foot pedal, John Paul Jones would later recall, 'Even in 1962 I can remember people saying, "You've got to go hear Neil Christian & The Crusaders, they've got this unbelievable young guitarist." I'd heard of Pagey before I'd heard of Clapton or Beck.'

1963

Jimmy Page:
BECOMES SESSION MUSICIAN AT DECCA

Within a year Page had made a big name for himself in London's musicians' circles and started jamming in The Marquee club with other British blues-boom legends Eric Clapton, Jeff Beck and Alexis Korner's Blues Incorporated (left). Following session work for a handful of EMI singles, Page would be offered regular work as a session musician for the Decca label. His first recording for them was on Jet Harris & Tony Meehan's 'Diamonds', a No. 1 hit in the UK. Though Page would briefly join Carter Lewis & The Southerners, he would leave the group almost as soon, preferring the 'impenetrable brotherhood' of the session-musician lifestyle. For a while at Decca, producers would solely call on either Big Jim Sullivan or 'Little Jim Page' to adorn their records.

1964

John Paul Jones:
BECOMES SESSION MUSICIAN AT DECCA

Moving in similar circles to Jimmy Page, and even playing on some of the same sessions as him ('It was always Big Jim and Little Jim,' Jones would say, 'Big Jim Sullivan and Little Jim and myself and the drummer ...'), in 1964 John Paul Jones would get regular session work with Decca, thanks to a recommendation from Tony Meehan. Just as Page would bloom on the guitar, it wasn't long before Jones would be arranger, bassist and keyboard player on plenty of mid-1960s' sessions, including recordings for Tom Jones (right).

Jimmy Page:
WORKS ON MARIANNE FAITHFULL'S 'AS TEARS GO BY'

With producers relying on Page's ability to mimic any guitar sound, the guitarist would find himself playing on sessions for artists as diverse as Marianne Faithfull (right) ('As Tears Go By'), The Kinks ('You Really Got Me'; 'All Day & All Of The Night') and even sitting in on Who sessions in case Townshend couldn't cut it playing lead in the studio (Page would still end up playing rhythm on their 'I Can't Explain'). Van Morrison's band, Them, would see some bad luck, as all members but Morrison himself were replaced by session musicians, including, of course, Jimmy Page.

1965

Jimmy Page:
WORKS WITH ANDREW LOOG OLDHAM'S IMMEDIATE RECORDS

Having taught himself the art of production with legendary engineer Glyn Johns, Page was sufficiently skilled to be hired by Andrew Loog Oldham (left) as house producer and something of a talent scout for Oldham's Immediate label. Working on, ironically, recording sessions for Chris Farlowe, Page would also produce Nico (the German chanteuse most famous for her work with The Velvet Underground) and John Mayall's Bluesbreakers, and record some jam sessions with Eric Clapton and Jeff Beck. By the end of the year Page would release a single under his own name, 'She Just Satisfies'/'Keep Movin'', though it failed to reach the charts.

1966

John Paul Jones:
WORKS ON DONOVAN'S 'SUNSHINE SUPERMAN'

During a Mickie Most session for Donovan's 'Sunshine Superman', John Paul Jones would take over, allegedly providing Most with a better rhythm arrangement than the hired arranger had provided. Impressed, Most hired Jones as a staff arranger and the bassist was soon working on sessions for Herman's Hermits and Lulu, along with further Donovan ones.

Robert Plant: FORMS BAND OF JOY

Having already played in blues and soul bands (one of which,
The Tennessee Twins, released a non-charting single: a cover of
The Rascals' 'You Better Run'), Plant joined Band Of Joy as
singer. Fired from them the following year (the manager thought
he couldn't sing), Plant formed his own Band Of Joy, an American
West Coast-influenced band in the mould of Love and Buffalo
Springfield. When they broke up Plant formed a third version,
which followed in the same direction, but with John Bonham
on drums. By the end of 1968, this Band Of Joy died without
being resurrected.

Jimmy Page: JOINS THE YARDBIRDS

By mid-1966, Page was stuck repeating himself over and over
on session work, simply hammering out formulas. Luckily The
Yardbirds, who had already asked Page to join them in 1965
when Eric Clapton was still in the group, approached him once
again. Jeff Beck (left) was now the lead guitarist but, despite
the psych-tinged hit 'Shapes Of Things', 1966 was proving to
be a tortuous year for the four-piece. Beck wanted to renew
the group's fortunes with Page, who was only too eager to
join, needing some energizing himself. The sonic possibilities
of Page and Beck's lead-guitar lines intertwining within The
Yardbirds were an opportunity too good to miss, though Page
would initially join the group as a bassist.

Jimmy Page: TOURS WITH THE YARDBIRDS

Though they boasted two lead guitarists, The Yardbirds toured
the States with Jeff Beck on lead guitar, and Page somewhat
restrained as their bassist. At one gig, however, Beck got a sore
throat and refused to play. Like a caged animal let loose, Page
assumed lead guitar duties for the night, while Yardbirds rhythm
guitarist Chris Dreja took over on bass. Letting out a torrent of
solos that perfectly mimicked Beck's – and even Clapton's –
old guitar lines, while being sure to throw in some guitar
histrionics of his own, Page offered the band a new lease
of life. It was no secret that The Yardbirds feared Beck's
departure, but in one night they found his replacement.

Jimmy Page:
STAYS WITH THE YARDBIRDS AFTER BECK FIRED

Ever since the August show, where Page replaced Beck on guitar for the night, tension had grown between the two guitarists. On tour in the US once more, Beck and Page each angled to hold on to a lead-guitar spot within a band that only needed one lead guitarist. Three days into the tour, Beck trashed his amps and guitar one night and walked off stage. The Yardbirds continued as a four-piece, with Page once again the lead guitarist. Though Beck apologized when the group caught up with him in Los Angeles, the three original band members opted to fire him. Allegedly Beck asked Page to come with him but Page, seeing a band he could take the helm of, decided to stay with the group.

Peter Grant: BUYS THE YARDBIRDS

While The Yardbirds finished their October US dates as a four-piece, their manager Simon Napier-Bell decided to sell them to promoter/manager Peter Grant. Though he couldn't save the group from deteriorating, Grant would learn a lot about the music business in the short time that he had them under his wing. Grant's hard-nosed, no-nonsense approach to management would allegedly see The Yardbirds make money on tour for the first time. Having proven himself an artists' manager (he would travel with the band and stay by their side at all times) Grant became one of the few people to have earned Jimmy Page's trust. His management of Led Zeppelin would make them one of the biggest, richest and most successful bands of all time.

John Paul Jones:
WORKS ON THE ROLLING STONES' 'SHE'S A RAINBOW'

John Paul Jones' session work had gone from strength to strength since he began working for Mickie Most (left), and in 1967 he would helm sessions for the likes of Jeff Beck and British rocker Terry Reid. The year would also see Jones record the most important session of his career so far when Andrew Loog Oldham, Immediate label boss and manager of The Rolling Stones, hired him to arrange the strings for 'She's A Rainbow', a future single from the Stones' forthcoming *Their Satanic Majesties Request* album.

John Paul Jones:
WORKS ON THE YARDBIRDS' LITTLE GAMES

Mickie Most was hired as producer for The Yardbirds' *Little Games* album sessions. Knowing too well that Most was interested in single material, but wouldn't give the time of day to album tracks, Jimmy Page was appalled. Of the actual band members he was the only non-session musician allowed to play, though Most wouldn't even let him hear the playbacks. Perhaps the only saving grace was that Most brought his usual arranger, John Paul Jones, along. Though Page and Jones had worked together on sessions before, being in a 'band' situation helped them to work together more closely.

1968-70

While all four future members of Led Zeppelin were busy laying the groundwork for their greatest success, Page got a major break playing for the ill-fated Yardbirds, a group that had already seen Eric Clapton and Jeff Beck move through its doors. When The Yardbirds finally dissolved, however, Page already had the bass-playing John Paul Jones' assurance that, when the time came, he would be ready to play with him.

As soon as Page went to see Robert Plant, a blues singer he had heard about, playing in Birmingham, he knew he'd found his singer. Through Plant, John Bonham was on board with this new group, and the four future members of Led Zeppelin played for the first time in September 1968. Before they knew it, they had a major label deal signed with Atlantic, would release three ever-more successful albums before the end of the decade and remain on the road for a year and a half, conquering America before they'd even played in England, gaining a reputation for being the most debauched, hedonistic rock'n'roll group the world had ever seen. With the blues as their jumping-off point, Led Zeppelin were soon straddling blues, rock and folk, while almost single-handedly creating heavy metal and writing some of rock'n'roll's most enduring anthems. With no politics or pretences, Led Zeppelin forced themselves into the world with music for the good times, bad times and all the times in between.

1968

January: THE YARDBIRDS' US TOUR

With Jeff Beck gone and Peter Grant now in the picture, Page had another 'more professional' ally with an active interest in The Yardbirds. It wouldn't be long before the group disbanded. Before that, however, Grant organized another tour of the US, this time hiring a young tour manager, Richard Cole (shown near left). Born in East London, Cole had been a roadie since 1965 and would quickly become as protective over Page and Led Zeppelin's interests as Peter Grant was. Essentially a one-man security system for Led Zeppelin, Cole would be the source (and often even cause) of many of their outrageous rumours. Alongside Grant, he contributed to the image that Led Zeppelin's business was run like a hardened East-London gangster's.

April: BAND GETS IDEA FOR ITS NAME

The source of Led Zeppelin's band name has never been entirely revealed. Some say Page was inspired by The Yardbirds' US contemporaries, Iron Butterfly, and their name, which juxtaposed a heavy substance with a light and airy object.

Other sources, however, claim that Richard Cole was given the idea when drinking in New York with John Entwistle (below) and Keith Moon of The Who, while The Yardbirds stopped off there on their US tour. Legend has it that Entwistle and Moon were complaining about their bandmates Roger Daltrey and Pete Townshend, and wished they could start a supergroup with Steve Winwood and Jimmy Page. Entwistle had supposedly joked, 'We'll call it Lead Zeppelin, because it'll f***ing go over like a lead balloon,' upon which Cole told Page of the idea as soon as he got back to the group. What most people do agree on is that Peter Grant convinced Page to drop the 'a' from Le[a]d Zeppelin, in order to stop people pronouncing it 'leed'.

Spring: ROBERT PLANT JOINS

After returning to England from their US tour, The Yardbirds
disintegrated. For Jimmy Page and Peter Grant, the hunt was
on for a new group, and that began with finding a new singer.
Someone had suggested to Grant that he check out a new band
called Hobbstweedle, fronted by a wailing blond blues singer
named Robert Plant. Page and Grant travelled to Birmingham
to see Plant in action and left knowing they'd found their man.
Page played it cool, apparently telling Plant only that he'd call
him within a week. Later, Page admitted, 'It just unnerved me
to listen. It still does. Like a primeval wail.'

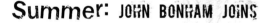

Summer: JOHN BONHAM JOINS

Plant had played with drummer John 'Bonzo' Bonham in the last
line-up of Band Of Joy, and knew the drummer well from
Birmingham musicians' circles. He had already tried to convince
Bonham to join the new group, but Bonzo was making enough
money playing for Tim Rose, and wasn't so keen on the risk.
When Page saw him in London, however, his mind was made up.
He *had* to have the driving sound that only John Bonham's
powerful drumming could provide.

Ever mindful of his artists' wishes, it's reported that Peter
Grant sent 40 telegrams to Bonham persuading him to join the
group. In the end, though, Bonham's acquiescence to join was
borne more out of musical preference. With other offers from
Chris Farlowe and Joe Cocker, Bonham chose Page's band
because it fitted the bill of 'which music was going to be right'.

September: FIRST REHEARSAL

The four members of Led Zeppelin have all unanimously described their first rehearsal as incredible. Plant would later say that he had 'never been so turned on in my life' when the group gathered for the first time playing old blues and rock'n'roll classics, and some Band Of Joy songs. Page felt so immediately comfortable that he would even try to teach them 'Dazed & Confused', a song that would appear on the first Led Zeppelin album, and which he had been toying with for a while since he joined The Yardbirds. The usually reticent Page would remember, 'We knew. We started laughing at each other. Maybe it was from relief, or from the knowledge that we could groove together.'

October: BAND BECOMES LED ZEPPELIN

Soon after their first rehearsal, Page, Plant, Jones and Bonham went on a European tour as The New Yardbirds, but they knew that they weren't the 'new' anything – these four musicians were nothing but themselves. Though the name wasn't as important as whether their music would be accepted, they quickly settled on Led Zeppelin, echoes of Richard Cole's tale and Iron Butterfly's heavy/light juxtaposition resounding in Page's mind.

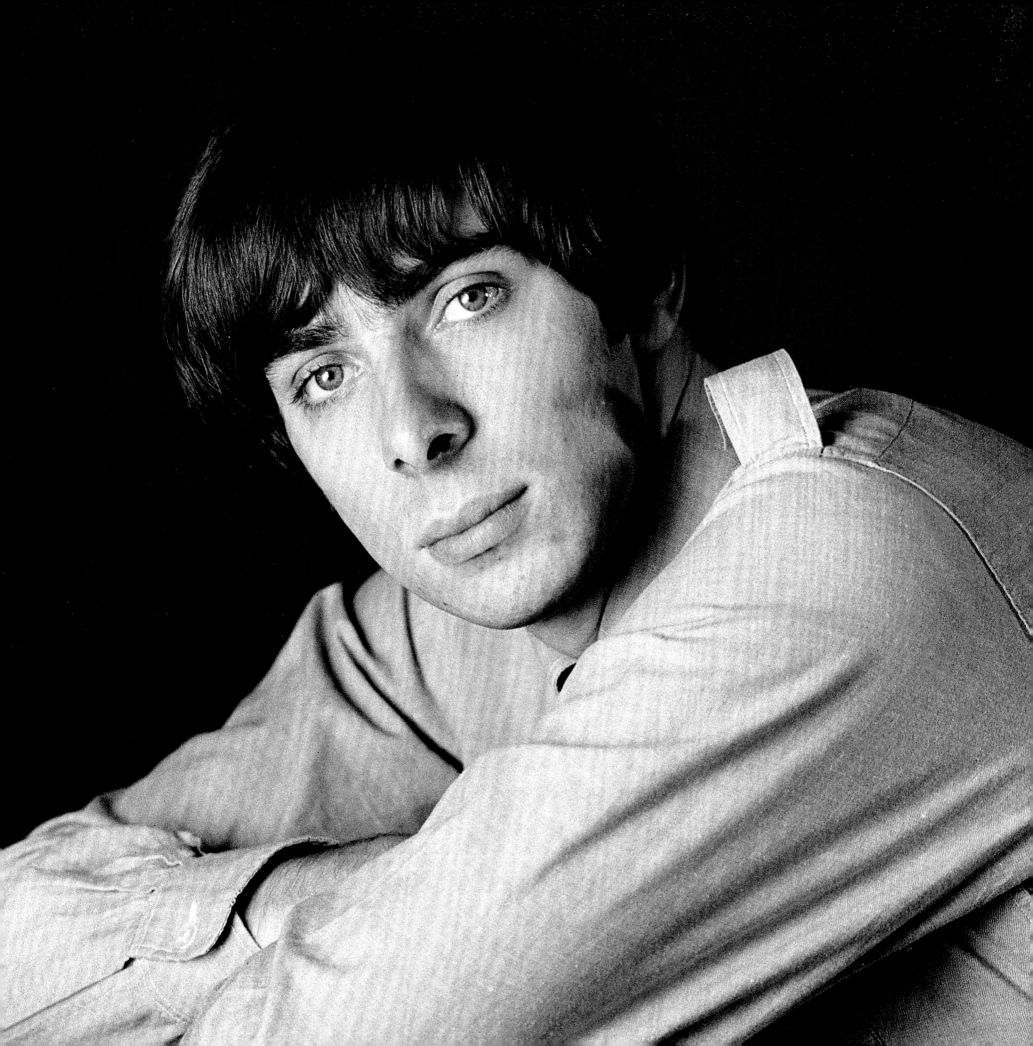

October: RECORD DEBUT ALBUM

Allegedly at a cost of just £1,750, Led Zeppelin recorded their first album in 36 hours across two weeks in London's Olympic Studios. The most experienced of the four, Jimmy Page would produce it, alongside Glyn Johns (left). For the most part a document of their European live show, the band intended for the record to be something they could sell while on tour in America during the coming months.

November: SIGN WITH ATLANTIC RECORDS

Peter Grant would win his greatest coup yet when he got the unknown and unsigned Led Zeppelin a record deal with the legendary Atlantic Records. Home to Stax Records and Muscle Shoals Studios, Atlantic was to Southern American soul what Motown was to Northern. Bypassing England entirely (and annoying both EMI and the Columbia-owned Epic, who had UK and US rights on The Yardbirds respectively), Peter Grant took the demos for what would become *Led Zeppelin* to Ahmet Ertegun (right) and Jerry Wexler at Atlantic. Demanding total artistic control and a record-breaking royalty figure, in return Grant signed the band to Atlantic for worldwide distribution. Led Zeppelin became the first rock band on the label.

November: LONDON DEBUT

On the same day that Robert Plant married his heavily pregnant girlfriend, Maureen, Led Zeppelin played their first London gig at The Roundhouse (they debuted the previous month at Sussex University, and soon enough were gigging in LA). The now legendary venue had already seen The Doors play there earlier in the year, but now it had a home-grown talent to celebrate. Not that it knew it. At this point the untried and untested Led Zeppelin were lucky to make £150 a night.

December: START US TOUR

Kicking off a near-straight 18 months on the road (including six different tours in the US alone), Led Zeppelin left London for Los Angeles in December. With Atlantic behind them, advance copies of the album spread the word to radio stations, which, in turn, spread the word to listeners. Playing for considerably less than The Yardbirds would have commanded, the group were just happy to be getting their music across. It wouldn't be long before early signs of their untold riches would come through, along with a reputation that would forever brand Led Zeppelin the most excessive and downright debauched rock group of all time.

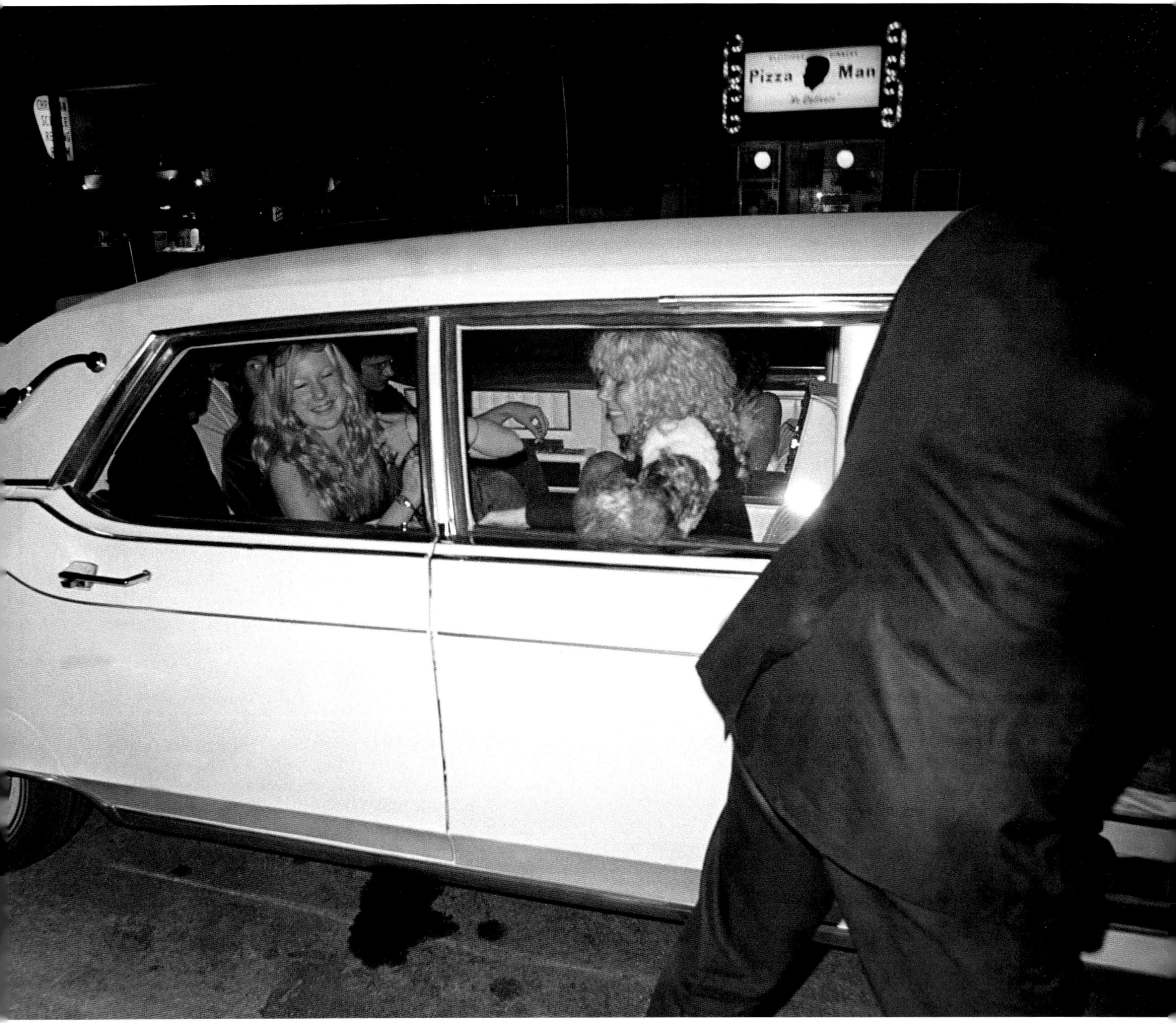
Pizza Man

1969

December: MEET THE GTOS

Before they had even played a gig, Led Zeppelin landed on Los Angeles' famous Sunset Strip with a bang. They immediately became the adopted rock group of legendary groupie contingent the GTOs (Girls Together Outrageously), the world's most famous set of 1960s groupies, who would even release their own album in 1969, *Permanent Damage*, produced by Frank Zappa. Though adhering to the more traditional aspects of groupie life, the GTOs would also offer the group something more like genuine companionship, providing them with the mother/lover/partner figures all in one while they toured the US West Coast.

January: ROLLING STONE SLATES LED ZEPPELIN

Despite great radio airplay, the US print media were lukewarm towards Led Zeppelin's self-titled debut. In an advance review, *Rolling Stone* magazine regarded Led Zeppelin as little more than 'an excellent guitarist … a competent rhythm section and a pretty soul belter who can do a good spade imitation'. Perhaps most galling for Jimmy Page was that the reviewer decided they weren't much better than the Jeff Beck Group. If Led Zeppelin fans were outraged (*Rolling Stone* is said to have been deluged with letters), Page and the group were even more so. The review led to a long-standing rift between Led Zeppelin and America's most famous music magazine: an early sign of both the negative response of the press to the band, and the band's equally negative approach to the media.

January: LED ZEPPELIN

Unlike most bands, who take a few albums to get into their stride, Led Zeppelin's self-titled debut, released in America on 12 January 1969 (the UK would have to wait until March), is one of the most important and envelope-pushing of all time. Many white British bands had been influenced by black-American idioms before, but none had made it gel as successfully as Led Zeppelin. Essentially introducing the group as four lead musicians in one band, Page's guitar work remodels blues standards such as 'I Can't Quit You Baby' into something harder and more metallic. Maybe not justifiably called the first-ever heavy metal album (there are far too many subtleties going on in the production; Plant's intuitive vocals are belted out, but with a control that most singers pray for; Page includes a mix of electric and acoustic guitars), *Led Zeppelin* (reaching No. 6 in the UK and No. 10 in the US) would foreground the thinking man's heavy metal. Most importantly of all, however, it contained a centrepiece in 'Dazed & Confused', a 6.26-minute opus that closed side one of the album and introduced Page's bowed guitar work, his instinct for creating atmospheric quiet-loud songs that never drag and a working band that were as tight a unit as any funk outfit. In short: Led Zeppelin could straddle British-blues boom and American psych, but not outstay their welcome.

January: SUPPORT IRON BUTTERFLY

On the final date of their US tour, 31 January, Led Zeppelin supported Iron Butterfly (right), though they might as well have been the headliners. With Jimmy Page resplendent in a red velvet suit, Led Zeppelin's two-hour set proved them infinitely better than the headliners, who were essentially living off of their 1968 hit single, 'In-A-Gadda-Da-Vida'. Iron Butterfly refused to go on stage afterwards and Led Zeppelin finished their first US tour as conquering heroes.

March-April: UK AND SCANDINAVIAN TOUR

If Led Zeppelin had conquered America, returning to England would soon help them forget that. As Richard Cole put it, 'You don't go on tour in England, you just went to work, doing your venues.' Led Zeppelin went from blowing headlining acts off the stage to slogging around in UK pubs. *Led Zeppelin* hadn't seen release until March, and Radio 1, the only radio station with any clout, wasn't even playing it. Though the underground press has its ears pricked by the album, this was a far cry from the support they had enjoyed in America. After their first and only UK TV appearance, plus some dates in Denmark and Sweden, Led Zeppelin returned to America.

April-May: US TOUR

Returning to America, quite clearly Led Zeppelin's spiritual homeland, the group were like caged dogs unleashed. Arguably, this tour alone gave them their reputation as debauched, disgusting, slightly scary rock'n'roll animals. Richard Cole later joked that they bankrupted one bar because they did not pay for their drinks. The band – all relatively young men with their first exposure to the rock'n'roll life – would quickly find out that anything goes when you're a rock star. And in late-1960s America, if you were a British rock star, then all the better. Girls would want to have sex with you, or with anyone (or anything) you may care to suggest. If rock'n'roll was the music of the devil, in less than six months Led Zeppelin had used it to turn America's teenage rock'n'rollers into wanton imps eager for the intense rush of seeing the loudest band in the world.

June: UK TOUR

Returning to England was not so much of a slog the second time. Led Zeppelin's notorious reputation preceded them, and the British press took this as a cue to take the band a bit more seriously. Instead of playing for a few hundred half-interested onlookers, Led Zeppelin would now be broadcast live on radio shows; perform at the Bath Festival Of Blues & Progressive Music; record some tracks for *Led Zeppelin II* and play such a long, intense, value-for-money show that, when they ran past the curfew time while headlining the opening night of the Pop Proms at London's Royal Albert Hall, they still returned for an encore, even though the staff had turned the lights off. If Led Zeppelin hadn't quite set the UK alight just yet, they had certainly given it something to remember.

July-August: US TOUR

On 5 July the Led Zeppelin storm continued to rage unabated. Their fifth tour (and third US tour) in just eight months, they returned to America for a summer-long stint taking in all manner of festivals and open-air appearances. The heady lifestyle of the past eight months was beginning to take its toll. Less than two weeks into the US tour, at the Singer Bowl on 13 July, a heavily drunk John Bonham started banging out a typical 'stripper's' drum rhythm, while proceeding to take his clothes off. By the time the police reached the stage, Peter Grant had already dragged Bonzo off it and back into the dressing room, telling him he was fired if his clothes weren't on before the police broke down the door.

July: 'RED SNAPPER INCIDENT'

Perhaps the pinnacle (or nadir) of Led Zeppelin's tour madness happened back at their hotel after a gig in Seattle. The Edgewater Inn was a popular Seattle hotel for rock groups, as it had a tackle shop in its lobby and you were free to fish from out of your hotel-room window. The facts are, as ever with drunken shenanigans, muddy to say the least. The legend sees Robert Plant, Bonzo and Richard Cole messing around on camera with a groupie and a red snapper. Rumour flies quickly and tales of lurid sex or, worse, rape, were soon on the streets and in groupie circles. Cole later recalled, 'It was nothing malicious or harmful … No one was *ever* hurt. She might have been *hit* by a shark a few times for disobeying orders, but she didn't get hurt.'

October: TOUS EN SCENE TV SHOW

On 10 October 1969, Led Zeppelin took to the stage at the Antelle Culturelle du Kremlin Bicetre to film two songs for the Parisian TV show *Tous En Scene*. Looking for all the world like a hippie band, but sounding like a extended battle cry, Led Zeppelin ripped into 'Communication Breakdown', with a slightly extended middle part, before tearing 'Dazed & Confused' apart and rebuilding it into a barely recognizable series of primal wails, spooky guitar effects and guitar notes rattled off like machine-gun fire. (Colour footage of these performances feature on the *Led Zeppelin* DVD released in 2003.)

October: PLAY LYCEUM THEATRE

Proving that the British had finally warmed to their homegrown talent, on 12 October Led Zeppelin were given the largest-ever fee up to that point for a British band to play for a single night. Perhaps it was in the cosmos. Almost 54 years to the day, on 13 October 1915, a German zeppelin had bombed the venue, London's Lyceum Theatre. Perhaps it's fitting that its namesake band used their appearance truly to stake their claim in Britain's musical heritage.

October-November: US TOUR

With the release of *Led Zeppelin II* imminent, the group returned to the States on 18 October for their fourth US tour within 10 months. If their first tour had lost the band money, this one would begin to bring them untold riches, especially when *Led Zeppelin II* was released. The Rolling Stones were also touring the States at this time, just prior to the release of their *Let It Bleed* album. Richard Cole caught a Stones show and reported that 'people were f***ing dead at the Stones' show, but the Led Zeppelin crowd was completely crazed. They were younger … and they still wanted to rock'.

October: LED ZEPPELIN II

Released on 22 October, *Led Zeppelin II* (No. 1 UK, No. 1 US) further strengthened the group's claim to being the most important, forward-thinking rock band on the planet, despite another derogatory review in *Rolling Stone*. Most bands recording on the hoof from America to England and back again wouldn't be able to keep up with the pace. Many have produced inferior albums when written on the road (The Beatles, of course, stopped touring to concentrate on their studio work), unable to come up with fresh ideas in such short snatches of time. Not so Led Zeppelin. If anything, their work strengthened.

More of a group effort, *Led Zeppelin II* (otherwise known as The Brown Bomber) furthered the ideas explored on their debut. The quiet-loud/acoustic-electric interplay was refined; 'Whole Lotta Love', containing one of the group's most enduring guitar riffs, would blueprint practically every hard-rock song to follow; 'Ramble On', with its questing nature and allusions to magic, brought the mystical into a genre that would come heavily to rely on the fantastical. Everything on *Led Zeppelin* had been enhanced and improved upon. With Page's production giving the album an even more distinctive sound than its predecessor, *Led Zeppelin II* earned its place as perhaps the group's first *bona fide* classic.

November: 'WHOLE LOTTA LOVE'

The enduring myth is that Led Zeppelin never released a single, preferring to have their albums viewed as a stand-alone body of work that couldn't be encapsulated in one song. It's a nice idea, but the truth is that Led Zeppelin singles have cropped up in all corners of the globe, in places as far flung as Angola, Ecuador and Venezuela. The first high-profile single release was 'Whole Lotta Love', released in the US and some European territories. Reaching No. 4 in the charts, the song quickly became US radio's favourite track off *Led Zeppelin II*, but at 5.34 minutes, it clearly broke the three-minute pop-song radio format. The radio stations made their own edits, cutting the extended middle-section jam out. The band baulked when Atlantic requested an official edited single version of the song, but the label won out, pressing up their own edited versions for promotional purposes, running to 3.10 minutes. The full-length versions of the song went out as a 7-inch single backed with 'Living Loving Maid (She's Just A Woman)', and 'Whole Lotta Love' became the band's only Top 10 US single, spending 13 weeks in the chart.

December: LED ZEPPELIN II REACHES NO. 1

It might have entered the charts at No. 199 in October, but The Brown Bomber soon made its mark. After climbing to (and spending a month at) the No. 2 position, the album went to No. 1 just before the close of 1969. Not only that, but in doing so it displaced The Beatles' *Abbey Road*. Now Led Zeppelin were the biggest British band in the States. If John Lennon had deemed The Beatles 'more popular than Jesus' in 1966, Led Zeppelin, with their gargantuan sound and all-conquering tours, must have seemed like gods on earth (in 1975, at the height of a 'me' decade, Robert Plant declared himself a 'golden god' from the balcony of his Los Angeles hotel room).

1970

January: UK TOUR

Lasting only a month, the most defining factor of Led Zeppelin's January 1970 UK tour would be the lack of support act. Only the biggest bands in the world could go on stage without a warm-up act preceding them, but Led Zeppelin had to drop something in order to stop the curfew problems their two-hour-plus shows were giving them. Without a support, Led Zeppelin were free to stretch out as they liked. John Bonham's solo drum spot, 'Moby Dick' (a mere four minutes long on *Led Zeppelin II*), would regularly stretch out to half an hour, while the group tore through blues standards and tracks from across their first two albums. (The entire Royal Albert Hall performance from 9 January, Jimmy Page's 26th birthday, is on the *Led Zeppelin* DVD of 2003.)

January: CHARLOTTE MARTIN

Meeting Charlotte Martin backstage at the Royal Albert Hall on 9 January, Page embarked upon a tempestuous relationship with the French model (and former girlfriend of Eric Clapton) that would see Martin mother Page's only child, Scarlet. After the January UK tour had ended, Page and Martin retreated to Page's Pangbourne Boathouse, where Page would withdraw from the rock'n'roll touring lifestyle. Never as outwardly excessive as his bandmates, Page became increasingly reclusive in his village home.

February: VON ZEPPELIN FAMILY

While rehearsing in Copenhagen for their European tour, Led Zeppelin were visited by Eva von Zeppelin, a descendant of Count Ferdinand von Zeppelin, inventor of the erstwhile zeppelin airship. Disgraced at the way in which she perceived the band was sullying her family's good name, she threatened them with a lawsuit if they appeared under the Led Zeppelin banner. Duly, the band's Dutch dates saw them play under the pseudonym 'The Nobs'.

February-March: SCANDINAVIAN AND EUROPEAN TOURS

On their first full-blown European tour, Led Zeppelin were confident enough in their stage show to begin introducing new material from the forthcoming *Led Zeppelin III* album to their sets. Everything continued apace, with the usual misbehaviour. At one press reception with an expensive modern art installation, Bonzo (as, Jekyll & Hyde-style, he was being increasingly known when he was drunk) took to redesigning some of the artworks that still had wet paint, and Peter Grant had to buy the pieces in question in order to appease the management.

March: THE FINANCIAL TIMES

A band is more than just a band when media coverage isn't restricted to the usual music press, tabloids or broadsheets; in the mid-1990s it would seem that David Bowie had more presence in the *Financial Times* than in the music press. Back in March 1970, Led Zeppelin would be the subjects of a feature in the world's leading financial paper, noting that the group stood to make $800,000 from 21 shows in a month-long US tour. For Plant this was an emotional godsend. Despite his achievements over the past year, his family scorned the rock'n'roll lifestyle their son had chosen for himself. With the *FT* feature, the singer gained a bit more stature in his father's eyes.

March-April: US TOUR

Led Zeppelin's fifth US tour proved to be more of a trial. They didn't have any problem selling out the shows or performing blistering live sets, but everything around the band turned a little bit darker. On at least one occasion Peter Grant (left) and Richard Cole had to use their gangster image to their advantage as they tried to combat bootlegging of the band's live shows. 1969 being a turbulent year for the US, the band had to travel from city to city while the country raged within its own borders at the height of public unrest over the Vietnam war. Death threats, armed guards, riots (and riot police) became a constant fixture at the live shows, and the band no longer enjoyed the wild freedom they had on previous visits. Their tour itinerary was planned to the minutest detail, something which began to drive them mad when they were confined to their hotels between shows.

April:

MADE HONOURARY CITIZENS OF MEMPHIS, TENNESSEE

The notoriously prejudiced southern states gave Led Zeppelin a hard time when they toured there. Whilst being refused service in some places thanks to their appearance, they even received some death threats. Amazingly, however, the band were made honourary citizens of Memphis, which meant that someone must have regarded them as important as the city's most famous resident, Elvis Presley. At the show on the night of 17 April, while the crowd were going mad over Led Zeppelin's set, the tour promoter threatened to shoot Peter Grant if he didn't take the band off the stage. With a laugh Grant reminded him that they'd just been given the keys to the city and that shooting him may not be such a good idea.

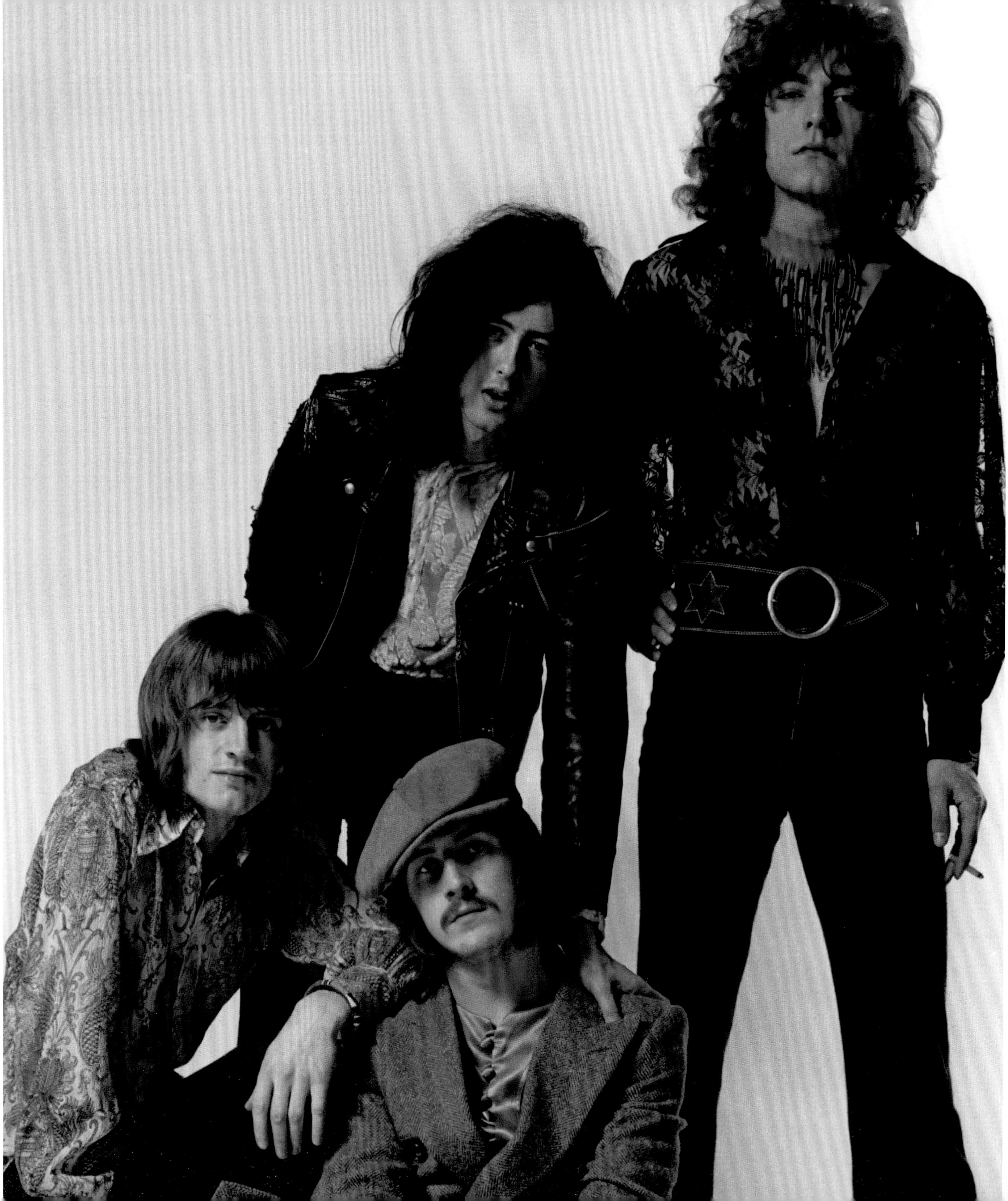

April: PAGE'S SOLO APPEARANCE

On 26 April 1970 Jimmy Page made an extremely rare solo
appearance on *The Julie Felix Show*. Recorded at BBC TV's Lime
Grove Studios in London, the performance saw Page returning to
his Bert Jansch folk and Spanish-guitar roots, as he played
'White Summer/Black Mountain Side' as a solo acoustic-guitar
piece. Page wasn't only looking back, though. His acoustic guitar
was to be more prominent than ever on Led Zeppelin's
forthcoming album in the same year.

May: BRON-YR-AUR, WALES

Needing a rest from what had been a year and a half of constant touring, Led Zeppelin got some well-deserved time off. John Paul Jones and John Bonham were able to go home and see their friends and family, but Page and Plant had to work on the follow-up to The Brown Bomber. Just as Bob Dylan, The Rolling Stones and The Beatles spent the turn of the decade getting back to their roots, so Page and Plant spent the beginning of the month ensconced in Bron-Yr-Aur, an 18th-century rural-cottage retreat in the mountains of Snowdonia, Wales. Relaxing in the countryside, with all the log fires and silent nights that entails, Bron-Yr-Aur would prove a huge influence on their more stripped-down, acoustic-based new material.

June: BATH FESTIVAL

With their new album recorded, Led Zeppelin performed their biggest UK concert yet on 28 June, to a record crowd of 150,000 at the Bath Festival Of Blues & Progressive Music. Grant had already turned down $250 million for shows in America on the same weekend, as he was determined that this would be his band's defining UK appearance, giving them a chance to upstage other acts on the bill such as Frank Zappa, The Byrds and Santana. Allegedly the group before Led Zeppelin, The Flock, began to overrun, but as Grant wanted Led Zeppelin to play with the sun going down behind them, he dispatched Richard Cole to pull the plug on The Flock. Naturally a fight ensued between both bands' camps, but Led Zeppelin made it on to the stage and performed one of the greatest shows of their career. Though it would be their last UK show of the year, it sent the group's profile into orbit, finally seeing them mentioned in the same breath as the likes of The Beatles and The Rolling Stones.

August-September: US TOUR

Playing similar shows to their Bath set in the UK, Led Zeppelin's sixth US tour would see them command over $25,000 a night on most nights (they would even see $100,000 for two shows at New York's Madison Square Garden – a far cry from the group that played for £150 just two years before). With nothing but their instruments and amps turned to ear-splitting volume, Led Zeppelin's two-hour-plus shows would see them run through material from their first two albums, plus new material slated for the third LP. With the group more than wise to the ways of the road now, it seemed that most of their worst excesses were behind them and that business was now conducted on a more normal (for rock'n'roll) level of management fights, alcohol abuse and the gig-hotel-gig treadmill.

September: 'ZEPPELIN TOPPLE BEATLES'

While the band were having a small break (with a few shows thrown in) in Hawaii, *Melody Maker*, perhaps the most influential of the UK music publications, printed the results of their latest readers' poll. The mob had spoken and Led Zeppelin were crowned best band, the first in eight years to usurp The Beatles' title. For his part, Robert Plant was awarded best male vocalist, while *Led Zeppelin II* was voted best British album.

ATLANTIC

K 50002 STEREO

October: LED ZEPPELIN III

Proving themselves no one-trick ponies, *Led Zeppelin III* (No. 1 UK, No. 1 US) came out on 5 October 1970 and went some way to throwing hardcore fans for a loop. With the phrase 'Do what thou wilt. So mete it be' (derivative of Aleister Crowley's philosophy of Thelema, 'Do what thou wilst shall be the whole of the law', which was not a manifesto encouraging people to indulge every whim, rather one that urged people to discover their 'True Will' and thus the divine reason for their existence) etched into the run-out grooves of side one of the vinyl, Jimmy Page was certainly doing what pleased him on this record. The album may have opened with 'Immigrant Song', such driving, frenetic rock as almost to be unplayable by humans, but its second track, 'Friends', was more akin to something from America's burgeoning West-Coast country rock scene, à la Neil Young or Crosby, Stills & Nash. Clearly Bron-Yr-Aur's relaxed vibes had an influence on the recording and *Led Zeppelin III* would be most notable for the way that the group could take the often-repetitive, sometimes lazy, folk-rock that was in vogue and make it as unmissable an experience as their harder, more immediately gripping recordings. It was panned by the press, though: the harder songs were seen as vacuous, more of the same; the acoustic tracks regarded as inauthentic blues from a bunch of style poachers.

Stung by the criticism, Page later cited displeasure at the album's artwork. Designed as a collection of disconnected images, it certainly served its eye-grabbing purpose. Its elaborate gatefold sleeve came with holes cut into the front. Behind this was a wheel device that the buyer could spin, thereby making different images appear in the holes. Page said that it was done in a rush, but maybe there was a deeper worry at the time that Led Zeppelin's acoustic music would need something more eye-grabbing to advertise it.

November: 'IMMIGRANT SONG'

Again against the band's wishes, Atlantic took the opening song from their new album and released it as a single. A somewhat ironic comment on immigration, Plant sung from the perspective of a Viking warrior conquering Western Europe. Its lyrics may have been a little laughable, but Atlantic obviously thought that its relentless, driving beat would make it a perfect sister single to 'Whole Lotta Love'. 'Immigrant Song' only managed to reach No. 16 in the US charts, however, its intensity and divide-and-conquer lyrics have since led to rumours that the song was played to American fighter pilots during bombings in the first Gulf War, though these have gone unsubstantiated.

Late 1970: BOLESKINE HOUSE

Long obsessed with the occult, Jimmy Page had become a collector of all things Aleister Crowley. Known as 'The Wickedest Man In The World', Crowley was a notorious English occultist. Practising occultist Page had amassed a collection of Crowley's books, manuscripts and personal effects, but purchased the ultimate Crowley artefact when he purchased his Boleskine House in Loch Ness, Scotland. Page would own the home into the 1980s and some of the fantasy sequences for *The Song Remains The Same* would be filmed in its environs.

December: 'STAIRWAY TO HEAVEN'

Still reeling from the criticism of *III*, Page set to work on what he intended to be Led Zeppelin's masterpiece. Needing something that would replace 'Dazed & Confused' as the band's centrepiece, Page intended to record 'something new with the organ and acoustic guitar building up and building up, and then the electric part starts', concluding that it 'might be a 15-minute track'. Page had already begun writing the song with Plant in Bron-Yr-Aur, and 'Stairway To Heaven' would be Plant's first attempt at writing lyrics for the band while out in Snowdonia in May.

Not only would 'Stairway' become their grandest statement, but it is also the most played rock song on US radio (despite never being released as a single) and the biggest-selling piece of sheet music in the world. The lyrics of 'Stairway' have long been open to interpretation, with many seeing it as the tale of one woman's quest for spiritual enlightenment, while Plant himself has called it a 'cynical aside about a woman getting everything she wanted all the time'. Page had certainly, unequivocally, succeeded in achieving what he set out to do. 'Stairway' was nothing short of a musical suite, with distinct movements shifting across the changing instrumentation. Now the best-known rock song in the world, when it appeared on Led Zeppelin's fourth album it was unveiled as a mini-opera the likes of which hadn't been quite so successfully realized since The Beatles recorded 'A Day In The Life' for *Sgt Pepper's Lonely Hearts Club Band* in 1967.

THE MID-LED ZEPPELIN YEARS: 1971-75

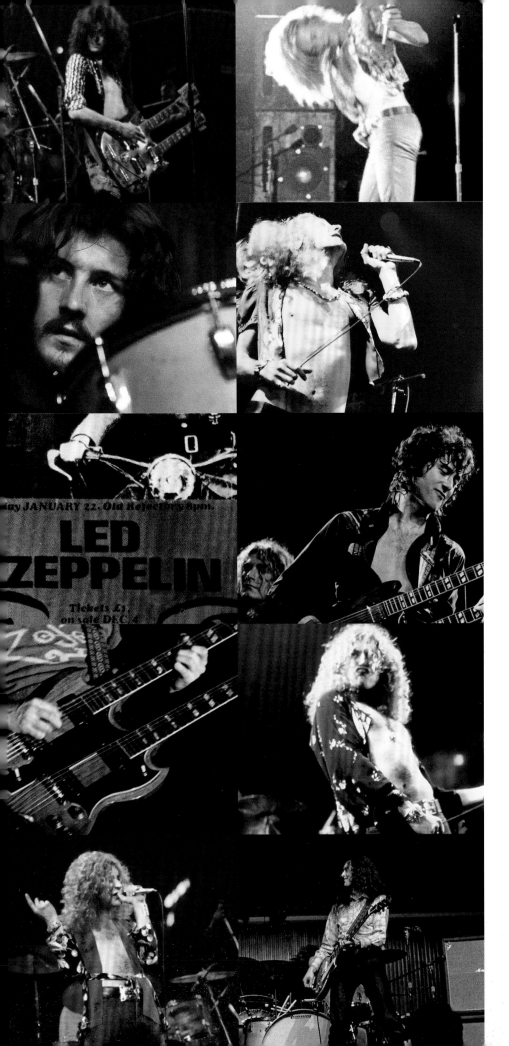

1971-75

If the 1960s had The Beatles versus The Stones, the 1970s had Led Zeppelin versus the world, and Led Zeppelin won. Frequently playing three-hour sets, their live shows became endurance tests for the band, and visitations from the gods for their audiences.

The first half of the decade would see the group outsell their label-mates The Rolling Stones; outrage America; become the most feared rock'n'roll group in the world; bring to rock music a sensibility that hadn't been seen in the genre before or since, and all of this without one iota of help from a press that would rather ridicule the band to failure than see them succeed.

In the 'me' decade, the 1970s, Led Zeppelin fitted the *Zeitgeist* perfectly, trashing everything in their way to further their cause and get what they wanted. It wasn't for nothing that they would frequently be viewed as a group with connections to the gangster underworld, but it worked in their favour. Led Zeppelin's manager, Peter Grant, rewrote the rulebook for bands on tour and make sure that Led Zeppelin earned and kept more money than those that had gone before them. And if anyone didn't like it, they were wise to keep their mouths shut. At their artistic and commercial peak, Led Zeppelin were untouchable in the first half of the 1970s, laying the foundations for a legacy that refuses to fade over a quarter of a century later.

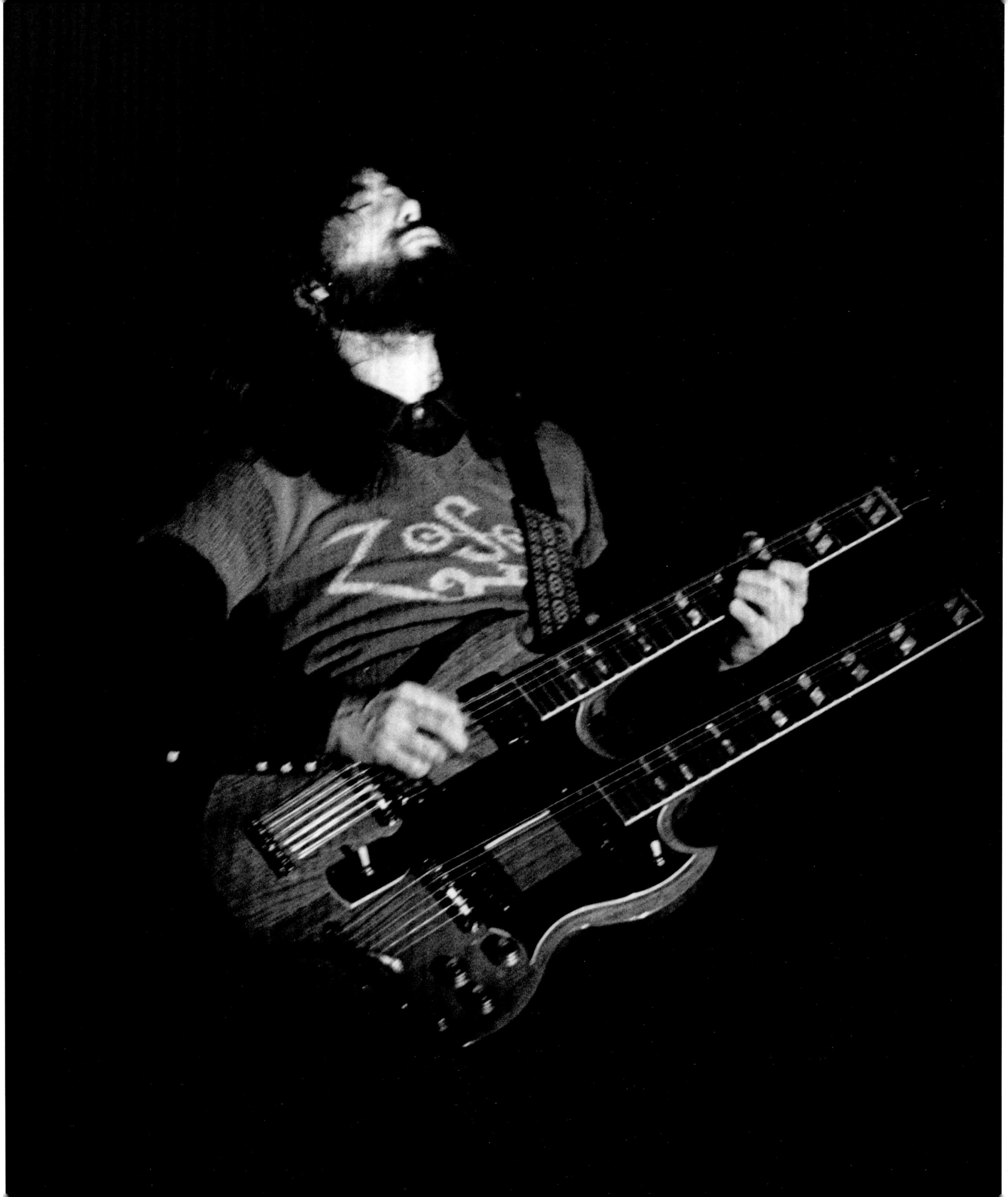

1971

March: IRELAND AND UK TOUR

For their Ireland and UK shows, Led Zeppelin played tiny venues in a 'back to the clubs'-style tour. Venues such as London's The Marquee and the Bath Pavilion had probably never seen such a group in its prime, but Led Zeppelin must have felt that they could use their more acoustic-based material to reconnect with an increasingly growing stadium audience. The shows weren't without their bombast, however, and in time for their first show in Belfast on 5 March (also the first time that Led Zeppelin had played Northern Ireland), Jimmy Page had his famous Gibson EDS-1275 double-necked guitar in tow, on which he would play 'Stairway To Heaven' live.

March: BONHAM THREATENS TO QUIT

After the Belfast show the band travelled to Dublin to stay overnight. Back outside the venue, Belfast was seeing the usual street riots of its own. Bonzo, as drunk as he was on Jameson's whiskey from the car journey, must have decided to take a little bit of it to Dublin, as he started a fight with the Intercontinental Hotel's head chef when looking for some late-night food. Richard Cole had to restrain him and ended up punching the drummer in the face, breaking his nose. That night Bonzo threatened to quit the band (at least giving some credence to the regular rumours *Melody Maker* had begun to print), though the incident was forgotten by the morning.

July: VIGORELLI VELODROMO

It was an inauspicious start for the band when they arrived to play at Milan's Vigorelli Velodromo stadium on 5 July. Armed riot police surrounded the venue and lined the inside, and the 12,000 fans had to stand through 28 other acts before Led Zeppelin were scheduled to take the stage. As Led Zeppelin's stage time drew nearer, the stadium got increasingly jammed with people, both backstage and out in the audience. Sensing that things could only get worse, Richard Cole forced the band on early to avoid the backstage crush, only to find that a literal riot awaited them on the other side of the stage door. At first the group attributed the smoke to fires being lit by the crowd, but it quickly became apparent that the armed police were attacking the audience with tear gas. As the set went on, the police forced their way forward and the crowd had no option but to surge on to the stage. Within a matter of minutes the group had fled, barricading themselves into a safe space, while their equipment got trashed.

August-September: CANADIAN AND US TOUR

It's estimated that, for the 20 nights that Led Zeppelin played across the United States and Canada, they would receive over a million dollars. By mid-1970 The Rolling Stones had signed to Led Zeppelin's label, Atlantic, and Led Zeppelin found out that they were outselling their great rock rivals three-to-one in the States. As far as the American audience was concerned, Led Zeppelin was the biggest band in the world.

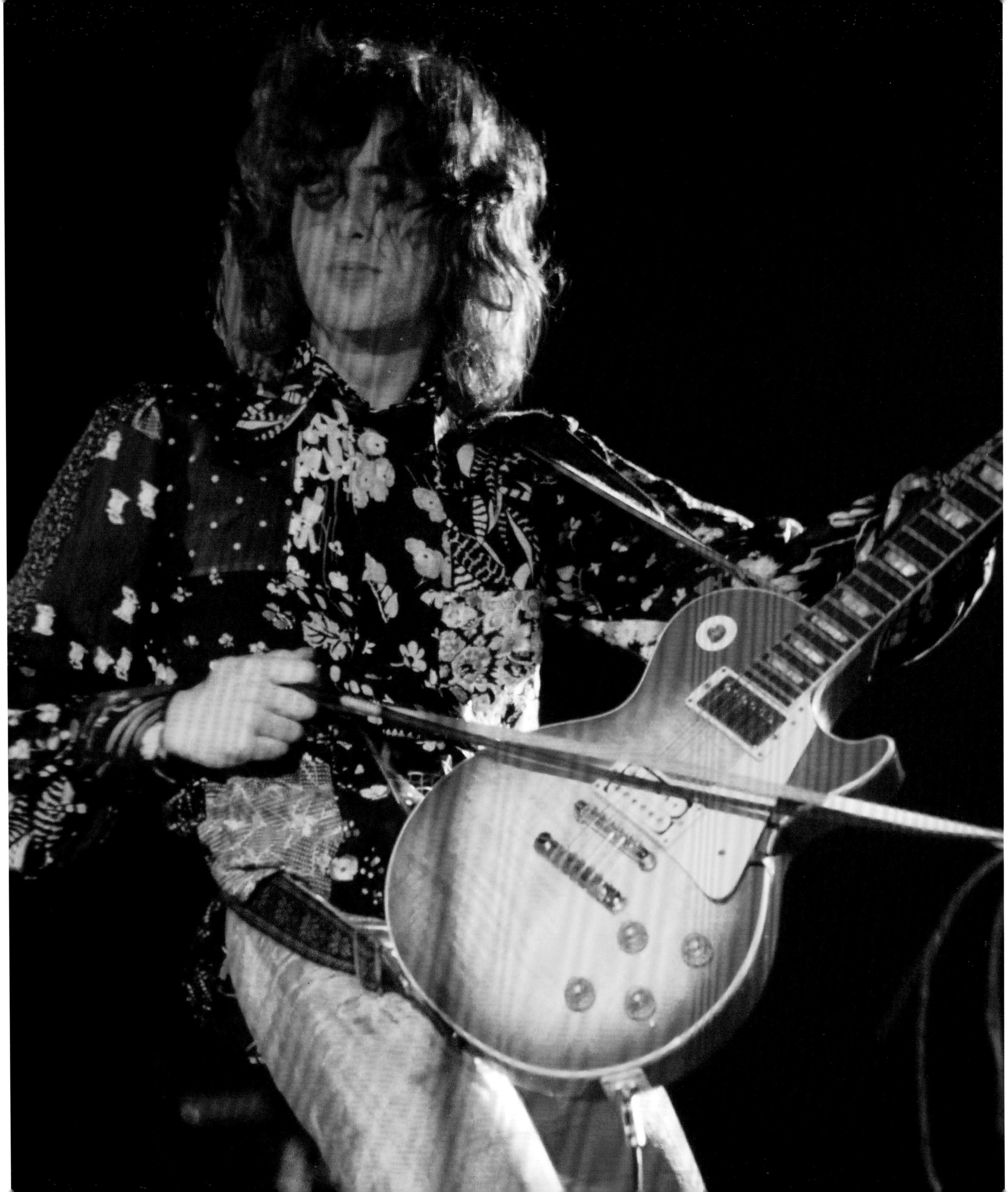

September: LIVE YARDBIRDS FEATURING JIMMY PAGE

Perhaps as a way of striking out at a band that Epic felt had left them for Atlantic, The Yardbirds' old label released *Live Yardbirds Featuring Jimmy Page* while Led Zeppelin were at the height of their US tour powers. Overdubbed with fake crowd noise, the live recording was of the Page-led Yardbirds on a really rotten night. Jimmy Page was livid and not a little worried at the effect such a recording would have on his reputation in his fans' eyes. Led Zeppelin's lawyers were deployed, and within a month the record was removed from the shelves.

September: JAPANESE TOUR

Playing in Japan for the first time, Led Zeppelin arrived like conquering heroes before they'd even played a note. 'Immigrant Song' was No. 1 in the Japanese charts and the group celebrated by earning themselves a lifetime ban from the Tokyo Hilton. Bonzo and Richard Cole had bought themselves samurai swords and used them to take their own, and their entourage's, hotel rooms apart.

November: LED ZEPPELIN IV

Reacting against the negative press that *Led Zeppelin III*
received, Page decided that their fourth album would have no
band information and no literal title. The music would speak for
itself and the album would be officially titled by four symbols.
Atlantic were incredulous: their biggest selling act were refusing
to even acknowledge their own presence on their own album and
Page wouldn't budge. They needn't have worried. The inclusion of
'Stairway To Heaven' made sure that the album topped the
charts at home and hit No. 2 in the States. A progression from *III*
(and receiving better reviews), the fourth album defines mid-
1970s heavy metal. From its more refined inclusion of mandolin
(a new instrument to Page) and lighter, acoustic passages ('Going
To California'); to the explosive rock that would climax the likes of
'Stairway', and see 'Black Dog' open the LP in a rabid frenzy, *IV*
defines Led Zeppelin at their most creative, while being the
blueprint for all heavy metal, of the mid-1970s or otherwise.

November: OCCULT REFERENCES IN LED ZEPPELIN IV

Page's obsession with Aleister Crowley and the occult was widely known, but making it so obvious on the fourth album's artwork was a move no-one anticipated. Atlantic wanted at least to have the band's name on the record-sleeve's spine, but Page decided that each band member could choose a symbol that best represented them. The symbols together would provide the official album's title, which fans later dubbed *Four Symbols*, *Runes* or *ZoSo* (after Page's symbol). While Page has never explained what his symbol means to him, it has been noted that it bears a similarity to the alphabet of the Magi, which was used for making talismans in the seventeenth century. Elsewhere the runes are also seen to reference the occult's favouring of 'threes' (Bonham's symbol of three circles intertwined), while Plant's refers to truth and justice. Perhaps reflecting Page's mind-set at the time, the front sleeve was dominated with the image of a hermit, which, in the Tarot, refers to taking a break and taking stock of one's situation before deciding to continue down the path travelled.

November-December: UK TOUR

Unusually, for a band of Led Zeppelin's stature, nothing much had changed in their live show, apart from the songs they played. *Led Zeppelin IV* songs would begin to dominate their live set in 1972 but, other than that, the group continued to play for hours on end with no support act. In a year where David Bowie – arguably Britain's second-biggest act, thanks to his success with *The Rise & Fall Of Ziggy Stardust & The Spiders From Mars* – was on the road defining glam rock with flamboyant make-up and costume changes, Led Zeppelin were still putting their audiences through their paces with endurance-test live shows, letting the music speak for itself.

December: 'BLACK DOG'

Perhaps engendering Led Zeppelin's wish to be an 'albums band', 'Black Dog' (backed with 'Misty Mountain Hop') became the second-worst selling of the band's US singles thus far ('Immigrant Song' stalled at No. 16), reaching a mere No. 15. The phenomenal album sales, however, suggested that the fans were buying the product the band wanted them to and ignoring the record company cash-in. With a stop-start riff courtesy of John Bonham, and a Robert Plant lyric mostly concerned with winning the lusty affections of a woman, 'Black Dog' was the kind of heavy rock number that Led Zeppelin could turn out on request these days. Instead of sounding tired and uninspired, however, it's one of the most recognizable and inventive of the heavy songs in the group's canon.

1972

January: LUCIFER RISING

It's fitting that, when one of cinema's most-noted avant-garde directors decided to make a movie reflecting his own interest in Satanism, he should ask the world's most-famous occultist to provide the soundtrack. Thus film maker Kenneth Anger asked Jimmy Page to provide the soundtrack to his new film, *Lucifer Rising*. Seemingly a match made in heaven (or hell), it would ultimately take Page more than three years to provide barely 20 minutes of music, which Anger felt was unusable. While it would not appear on the film, Page self-released it as a blue vinyl album in 1987, on his own Boleskine House Records.

February: AUSTRALIA AND NEW ZEALAND TOUR

A band in Led Zeppelin's position could afford to take a break but, instead, they continued touring as though they had just landed in Hollywood in 1968. Their first tour of 1972 was meant to start in Singapore, but the Singaporean authorities refused the band entry into the country because of their long hair. After briefly returning to London, they were able to tour Australia and New Zealand.

March: PAGE AND PLANT VISIT INDIA

Taking a break following their tour of Australia and New Zealand, Page and Plant returned to India for the first time after a brief visit the previous year. Page had long been looking to blend Western and Eastern music styles and held an experimental recording session in Bombay with some local musicians. This Eastern influence would ultimately find its way on to *Houses Of The Holy*, most notably in 'The Song Remains The Same', Page's tribute to world music.

June: CANADIAN AND US TOUR

If Led Zeppelin hadn't already moved the goal posts for stadium tours, their Summer US tour of 1972 would see manager Peter Grant changing the rules forever. In the early 1970s the music business still adhered to 1950s and 1960s tradition: a band would split the profit from ticket sales 50-50 with the promoter. Grant, however, decided that this wasn't good enough for his band. Led Zeppelin were the artists, the tickets were being sold on the back of their talent, and so they should get 90 per cent of the gate. Grant's revolutionary business style would see Led Zeppelin earn more money for themselves than any other touring band up to that point.

June: LORI MADDOX

A surprising, but prominent, character in the Led Zeppelin story, Lori Maddox was just 14 when Jimmy Page met her in June 1972. Maddox was a teen model at the time, when Led Zeppelin's then-press officer, B.P. Fallon, had shown Page a picture of her. Page was smitten, all but giving up his current relationship with Pamela Des Barres, essentially the leader of the GTOs, to date Maddox in the US, while also living with Charlotte Martin at home. Their affair would last for years, being sometimes secretive, other times almost too open for comfort. Maddox would maintain that their romance was so strong they fell in love, while Page, compared to most rock stars' behaviour, treated Maddox like a princess.

October: JAPANESE TOUR

Led Zeppelin's second tour was business as usual, with a few 1950s classics thrown into set lists, including B.B. King's 'Stand By Me' one night. The band got bored part way through the tour, however, and took a break in Hong Kong, while also seeing if they would be able to play there. By now, breaking into new territories was becoming more interesting to the band than playing to the same old crowds.

1973

March: HOUSES OF THE HOLY

Fittingly for an album that didn't continue in the tradition of Roman-numeral-titled albums (overlooking the variously titled *ZoSo*, *Led Zeppelin IV* and *Fourth Album*, of course), *Houses Of The Holy* (No. 1 UK, No. 1 US) saw probably the biggest stylistic shift in Led Zeppelin's recording career. Though the blues and heavy rock were present, they were no longer such overt forces. Songs such as 'The Crunge' and 'D'yer Mak'er' would see Led Zeppelin try on funk and reggae respectively, while John Paul Jones would bring, in the core of 'No Quarter', one of the moodier tracks in the Led Zeppelin canon. It might have seemed as though the band's collective mind was wandering, but the diversity actually led to a Led Zeppelin album which, though it has its serious moments, also sounds as if it could be the one they had the most fun recording.

December: UK TOUR

Led Zeppelin's UK tour lasted until January 1973 and was the biggest UK tour they had put on up to that point. The 120,000 UK-wide tickets sold out in 24 hours, covering dates across England, Scotland and Wales. This tour saw one of their strangest gigs, playing for a seated, formally attired audience in Kings Hall, Aberystwyth, Wales. Some dates were postponed thanks to Robert Plant catching a cold, but other than that, it was much as always, with three-hour shows on stage and Bonzo trashing hotels off stage.

THE EFFECT IS SHATTERING...

March-April: SCANDINAVIAN AND EUROPEAN TOUR

Led Zeppelin's tour of Scandinavia and Europe across March and April 1973 was mostly characterized by riots and the band tearing France up as they toured through five of its major cities. On one occasion, a hotel in Nantes saw two of its floors flooded after Robert Plant was unable to get any milk for his tea. Throughout the tour John Bonham's split-personality like behaviour became more pronounced. The charming John Bonham was not the same creature as Bonzo, who would smash up backstage areas and hotels at the drop of a hat. It was during this tour that he picked up a second nickname: The Beast.

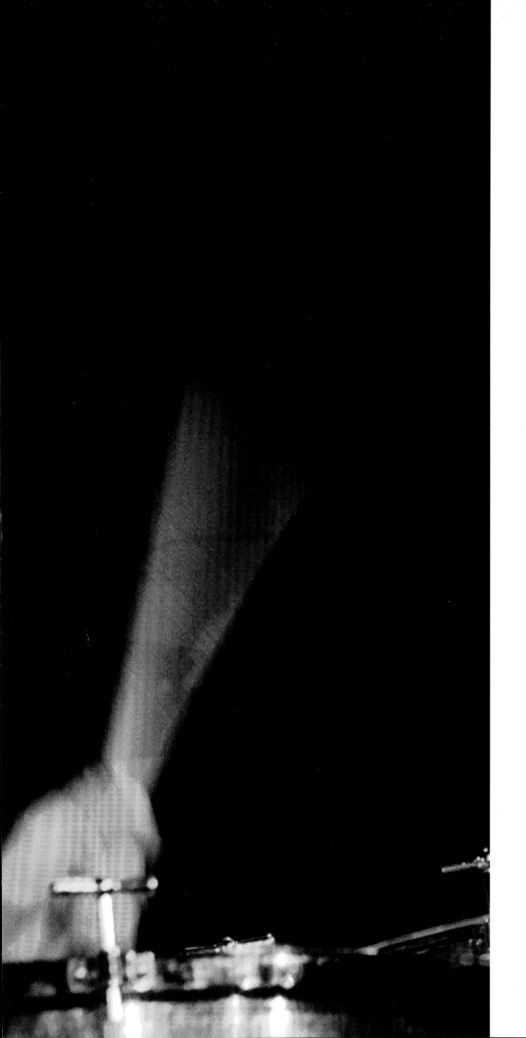

April: PRESS AGENTS APPOINTED

Though the group (including Peter Grant and Richard Cole) had no small degree of pride in their Neanderthal-like image, even Grant had to concede that it was perhaps beginning to dog them. Other than from afar, the press were largely too scared to approach the band, or uninterested in what they saw as a two-dimensional story of rock'n'roll excess. Led Zeppelin's early tours in America had given them a reputation that, come 1973, they were beginning to find an albatross. Though Grant had hired a press agent, B.P. Fallon, in June 1972, he would hire Lee Solters and Danny Goldberg to replace him in April 1973, feeling the band needed a bigger push (Solters also represented Frank Sinatra, of all people). With the agents on board even Bonham gave pause for thought, telling them, 'We're the biggest and the best and no one knows it. You gotta do something about this.'

May-July: CANADIAN AND US TOUR

At the same time as hiring their press agents, the group's US touring kicked into overdrive, suggesting that they were on an all-out campaign to win the attention of the press. Partially to satiate Page's fear of flying, undoubtedly partially to promote their status, Led Zeppelin began flying in their own privately chartered jet, *The Starship* (right). The aircraft was so luxurious for the time that it was practically an airborne hotel. When on ground, Grant would hire out entire floors and sections of hotels for his group to stay in. Led Zeppelin were rumoured to be making $30 million this year, and most of it was coming from this 33-date tour.

If it was a media furore they wanted, it was a media furore they got. All of a sudden the group were asked to be on the cover of *Rolling Stone* (the very magazine that had taken such pleasure in trashing their earlier albums), and given plenty of TV offers – all of which they were powerful enough to turn down.

May: TAMPA STADIUM

With *Houses Of The Holy* having just knocked Elvis Presley's *Aloha From Hawaii* off the top spot in the albums' chart, Led Zeppelin were about to outdo another of rock's sacred cows – for the second time. Led Zeppelin's 56,000-strong crowd in Tampa, Florida, broke The Beatles' eight-year record for one single act attracting the largest-ever audience at a concert. Eight years before, in 1965, The Beatles played Shea Stadium to 55,000 paying fans, taking in $301,000 for their trouble. Not only would Led Zeppelin attract an extra thousand fans to that number, they also grossed an extra $8,000.

July: MADISON SQUARE GARDEN

It had already been mooted that some of the US dates should be filmed for a tour film, but it wasn't until the three Madison Square Garden, New York, dates, which closed the US tour, that a film crew was assembled for the purpose. Filming went inauspiciously, however, as the crew had some problems filming the group's longer songs, and John Paul Jones wouldn't wear the same clothes for three nights in a row, making continuity a problem. If filming wasn't trying enough for a band that just wanted to play, on the last night of the tour they lost an estimated $200,000 in cash from their hotel safe. Understandably, the band and their entourage were fuming and the FBI involved, but the culprit was never caught and the money never seen again.

September: 'D'YER MAK'ER'

With a title punning on the British way of saying 'Jamaica' (as the old joke goes: 'My wife's gone to the West Indies.' 'Jamaica?' 'No, she went of her own accord.'), 'D'yer Mak'er's reggae influence gave the song a catchy appeal to fans of *Houses Of The Holy*. While critics saw it as a throwaway track on the album, Robert Plant himself was apparently eager to have it released as a single in the UK. Promo copies were allegedly pressed up for radio play, but the single proper never materialized in the UK. It would, however, be released in Peru, Spain and Yugoslavia, each time with 'The Crunge' as the B-side.

Do what thou wilt . . .
But know by this summons
That on the night of the Full Moon
of 31st October, 1974

Led Zeppelin

request your presence
at a
Halloween Party
to celebrate
Swan Song Records'
first U.K. album release
'Silk Torpedo'
by

The Pretty Things

in

Chislehurst Caves,
Chislehurst, Kent.
Celebrations will commence
at 8.00 p.m. . . . .

Swan Song Records

Distributed by Atlantic Records

1974

May: SWAN SONG

1974 was a relatively quiet year for a band that had spent its life touring, though the group would up their business activities when they launched their Swan Song label in May. Compared to The Rolling Stones, who launched their own label under Atlantic the previous year, Swan Song would be a complete working entity. Led Zeppelin approached their label in a similar way that The Beatles had done with Apple, signing bands such as Bad Company (whose self-titled album would be the first US Swan Song release in June), Maggie Bell and The Pretty Things (whose *Silk Torpedo* would be the first UK release in October), while also putting out their own albums under its banner.

1975

January-March: CANADIAN AND US TOUR

Come the end of the previous year, Led Zeppelin realized that the tax man would soon be taking home more of their money than they would. They had no choice but to enter into tax exile in 1975, beginning with a tour across the US and Canada that would, they planned, see them continue out on the road worldwide for the entire year. Page injured a finger on his left hand before even leaving England, though: a bad start to a tour that wasn't their best. The group brought laser light effects on the road with them for the first time, which helped to cover up some of the lesser moments on stage. Starting under the cloud of tax exile, the tour would really be the beginning of the end for the band, with some gruelling four-hour shows and a near plane crash that added to the quick drop in morale when homesickness set in.

February: PHYSICAL GRAFFITI

For a band so often accused of being self-indulgent, it took them seven years to release their first double album, and *Physical Graffiti*'s (No. 1 UK, No. 1 US) diversity recalls the initial forays into new territory that *Houses Of The Holy* saw. While some of it can pass by unnoticed, the overbearing presence of synthesizers demanded the listeners' attention, as did the obvious Eastern influence of 'Kashmir', this album's anthem, the beast-let-loose blues-metal of 'Trampled Underfoot' and Led Zeppelin's longest studio-recorded song, the 11-minute-plus intense blues rock of 'In My Time Of Dying'. There were a few throwaway scraps and odds-and-ends included (going as far as back as 'Bron-Yr-Aur', a *Led Zeppelin III* outtake), but the fans didn't notice, sending the album (the band's first own release on Swan Song) to the top of the charts on both sides of the Atlantic. February 1975 would see nine Led Zeppelin-related albums in the US charts: six of their own, with three more coming from their Swan Song artists.

March: BONZO'S MENTAL STATE

Perhaps reflecting his state of unhappiness at the time, John Bonham had taken to wearing the white boiler suit and black bowler-hat uniform made famous by Stanley Kubrick's notorious *A Clockwork Orange* film. The 'ultraviolence' perpetrated by the film's anti-hero, Alex de Large, seemed to resonate with Bonzo, who was getting more and more out of hand when he drank, attempting to numb the pain of not being able to see his family because he was in tax exile. One particular incident saw Bonzo attack a journalist from *Sounds* magazine – after he had told Bonham that he was the greatest drummer in the world. Bonzo's rationale was that he'd taken enough hostility from the press in the past, but this was sadly just one event in a string of physical attacks that took place as Bonham's condition deteriorated more and more on the road.

April: 'TRAMPLED UNDERFOOT'

Rumour has it that only 5,000 copies of the 'Trampled Underfoot'/'Black Country Woman' single were pressed in the UK, but other sources refute this, claiming it to be the easiest UK Led Zeppelin single to find. Atlantic approached the group to release a limited-edition run of the single for record dealers only, as a way of encouraging them to stock up on Led Zeppelin albums in time for their Earls Court dates in May. For every 20 albums bought, the dealers would receive five of the new 7-inchers to do what they liked with. Given the limited nature of the single, it didn't chart. There are some expensive rarities, however, including a mispressing featuring The Pretty Things on the B-side, and a handful of test pressings that Led Zeppelin collectors would pay close to £2,000 for.

May: EARLS COURT

Presenting a more relaxed group than the one that had just toured America, Led Zeppelin's five Earls Court shows were a real homecoming for the band that weren't able to live at home. Though they took the laser light-show with them, here it didn't need to cover for any drops in quality as the group performed some of the best shows of their career (footage of the show on 25 May can be found on the *Led Zeppelin* DVD). The residency was such a celebration, in fact, that Jeff Beck even joined them in their backstage party after the final show and the *Observer* would claim that Led Zeppelin had 'propelled rock'n'roll into the forefront of artistic achievement in the mid-70s'.

August: ROBERT AND MAUREEN PLANT'S ACCIDENT

After a touring break involving a Moroccan trip to record more indigenous music, Page, Plant and their respective families (Charlotte Martin and Robert's wife Maureen, plus both couples' children) took a summer holiday to Rhodes, the Greek island. Page took a vacation from the vacation when he went to Sicily to see an old farmhouse of Aleister Crowley's, which he heard was going on the market. The following day, while driving a hired Austin Mini, Maureen Plant lost control of the car and crashed into a tree. Plant suffered a series of injuries along the right side of his body and his children were wounded, while Page's daughter, who was also in the car, got off lightly. Maureen, however, suffered a fractured skull and a broken pelvis, and needed a blood transfusion that wasn't available in Rhodes. Luckily, word got back to Peter Grant and Richard Cole, who were able to use Led Zeppelin's considerable finances to get everyone out of Greece and back to British medical aid. Plant, however, would have to be taken to Jersey to continue his tax exile, while the band's 1975–76 tour was cancelled.

December: 'ACHILLES LAST STAND'

As was quite clear by now, every Led Zeppelin album would have its epic masterpiece, and the song which opened 1976's *Presence* LP, 'Achilles Last Stand', was no different. Based on Page and Plant's summer holidays in Morocco, Plant, who was recording from the disadvantage point of a wheelchair thanks to his broken leg, was surely aware of the similarity between his and the Greek warrior Achilles' injuries. With such pent-up tension, the band went all out on this one: Bonham's drumming is some of his most ferocious on record, Jones used a custom-made eight-string bass, while Page would multi-layer the guitar tracks even more than usual. He also changed the tape speed during the mixing, something which he rarely ever did, giving the song a feeling unlike any others in the Led Zeppelin canon. Page has singled 'Achilles' out as being his favourite Led Zeppelin song, and it would feature in the set list of every tour after *Presence* was released.

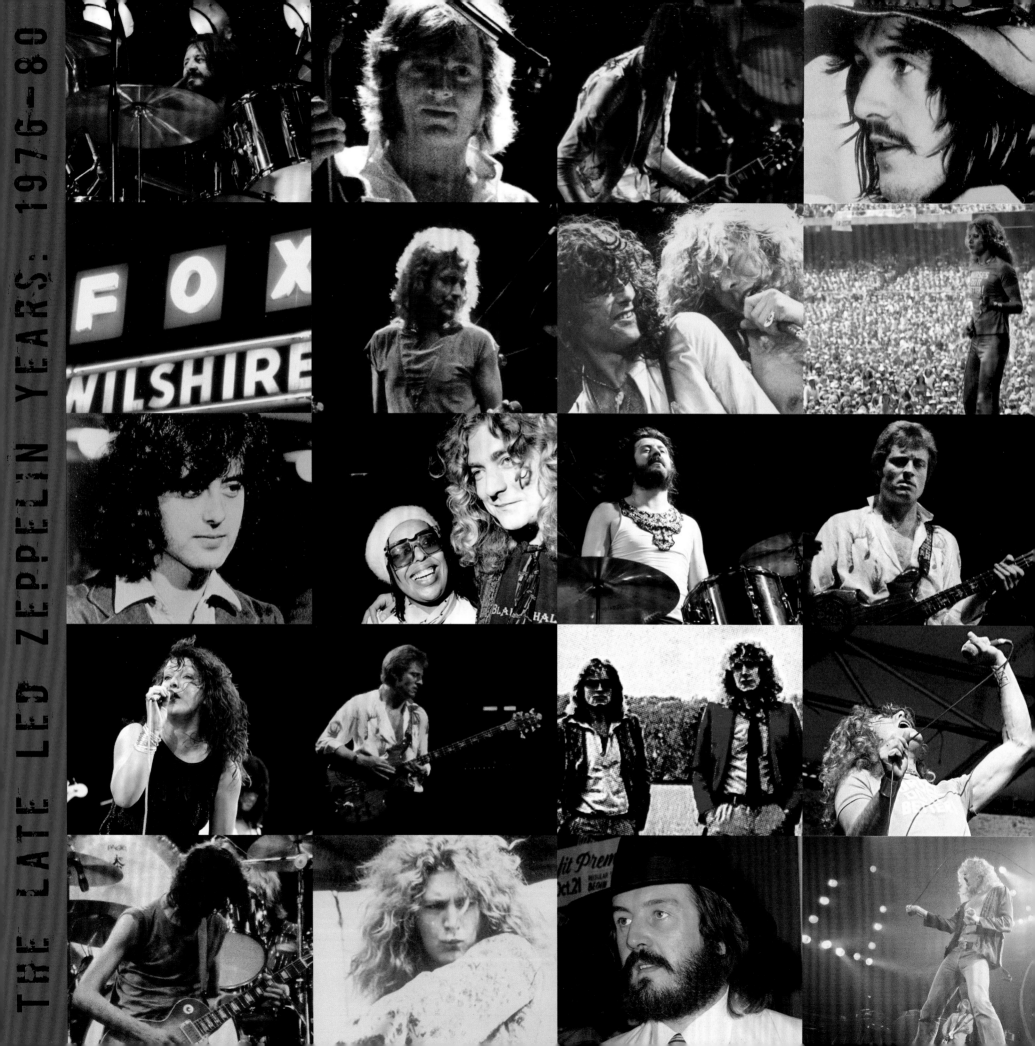

THE LATE LED ZEPPELIN YEARS: 1976-80

1976-80

Led Zeppelin had spent the first half of the decade turning themselves into the greatest rock'n'roll band in the world. Not even the onslaught of punk could see them fail to sell out Knebworth on two weekends running in 1979. But they had a long way to fall, and a series of bad-luck events saw the Led Zeppelin empire crumble. Some said it was a karmic pay-back for Jimmy Page's dabblings in the occult and black magic.

Within the space of five years Robert Plant would have a near-death experience when he was involved in a car crash while on holiday with his family; the group would release their first disappointing album; Jimmy Page would be seen struggling under an alleged heroin addiction; John Bonham would quickly begin to lose the grip on his nicer side, as touring commitments made him more despondent, at times seeing him lash out at anyone around him.

It could have all just been coincidence, however, but when John Bonham died on 25 September 1980, aged just 32, Led Zeppelin as the world knew them were over. Though each member would be heard from again – solo and as a group – the driving voice behind their music was silenced forever.

1976

March: PRESENCE

It had to happen sometime. Perhaps it was a combination of the stress and tension following Plant's car crash and his wife's near-death; the fact that the band knew they should have been on the road; the depression of remaining in a tax exile that prevented them from going home; or that it was recorded and mixed in just 17 days, but *Presence* (No. 1 UK, No. 1 US) was the first below-par Led Zeppelin album. The band themselves seemed to acknowledge this, as they only played two of the album's tracks live, 'Achilles Last Stand' and 'Nobody's Fault But Mine'. While previous albums had had their 'throwaway' tracks, at least they were *good* throwaways. *Presence*'s problem was that, despite epic pieces of good quality and a tangible menacing feel, the shorter tracks didn't have much to offer, seeming like half-baked ideas. Again the album's artwork attracted great attention, thanks to the use of a black obelisk-like image referred to only as 'The Object'. Pictured in places as diverse as a family dinner table, a golf course and a school, 'The Object' took on more significance in fans' minds than the band intended, and it has given way to much rumour and theorizing over what its ominous presence could mean.

September: BONZO LASHES OUT

While Led Zeppelin the group was struggling to remain on top in 1976, John Bonham the man was battling to retain control of the beast. Ever since his daughter Zoe had been born in June 1975, Bonham was becoming increasingly more despondent when he was away from his family. Having recently spent the summer with them in the south of France, when they returned to England Bonzo moved on to Monte Carlo with Richard Cole and friend Mick Hinton. It was probably no surprise that Bonzo would lose it before long and on one night out he went mad at Hinton for a long-forgotten reason, hitting him with a gas gun that he carried with him. Unfortunately the club was full of gangster types and Cole had to break Bonham's nose for the second time in five years to stop him from getting anyone into some even more serious trouble.

October: THE SONG REMAINS THE SAME

If, perhaps, *The Song Remains The Same* film and accompanying soundtrack were intended to remind Led Zeppelin fans of the group's incredible stage show after the disappointment of their studio LP *Presence*, the soundtrack album brought to mind something different. There are a few songs from the film not on the soundtrack, and some versions of songs on the soundtrack differ to the ones in the film. Regardless, though, *The Song Remains The Same* (No. 1 UK, No. 2 US) is one of the most boring live albums any band could have released. Recorded at the same July 1973 Madison Square Garden shows that were filmed for the tour movie, it seems that the group may have been more concerned with looking good than sounding great. Though long solos and extravagant reworkings of their classics were *de rigueur*, on these nights they were uninspired, indulgent and more of a chore than a pleasure to listen to. 'Dazed & Confused' alone took up one whole side of the double-vinyl release. Sadly for the band, *The Song Remains The Same* was not the way they should have marked their live shows for posterity.

October:
THE SONG REMAINS THE SAME PREMIERE

Two days after the release of the film's soundtrack LP, *The Song Remains The Same* movie was premiered in New York. If its accompanying album was evidence of a band in indulgence mode, the film was unbearably self-obsessed. The band had played it up on stage enough in Madison Square Garden, but the inclusion of a series of 'fantasy' sequences intercut between songs just saw them ending up with a messy, aimless film. The fantasy sequences were intended to give an insight into each band member's personality, but instead it just suggested that they were full of more self-importance than had originally been thought.

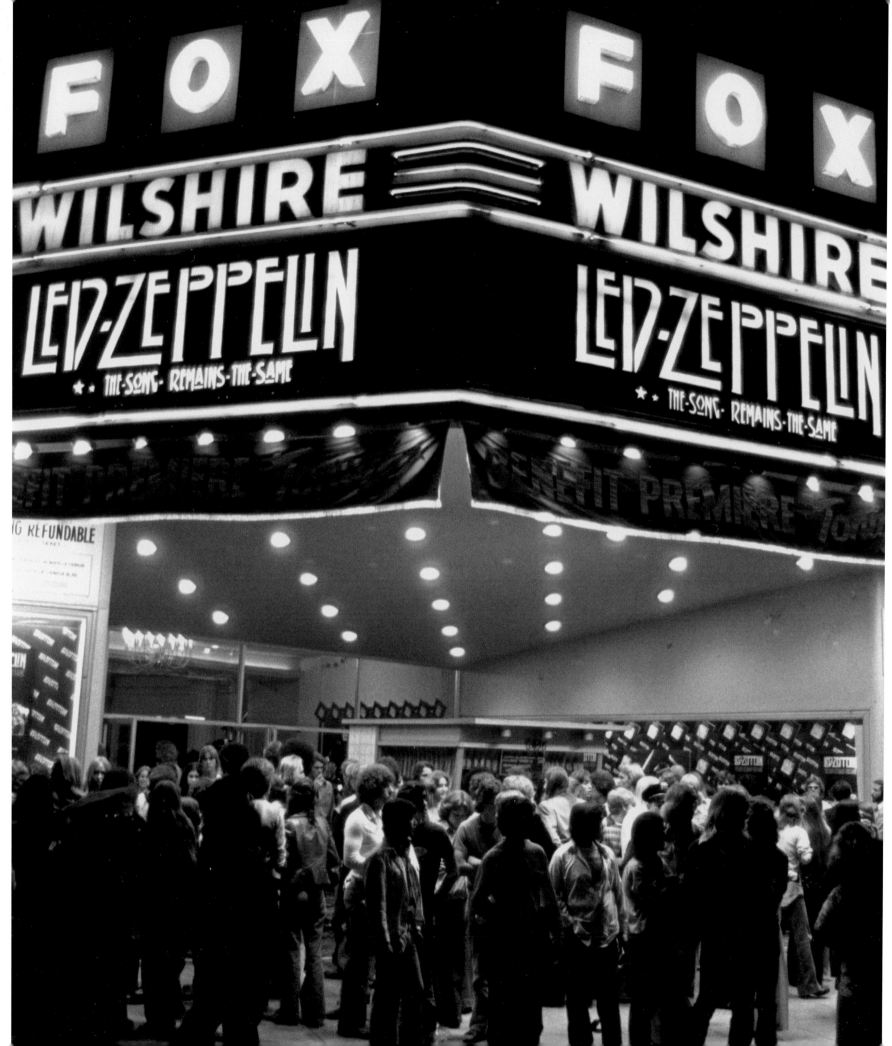

1977

April-July: US TOUR

If, by 1977, punk had seemingly launched itself into the music scene and wiped away all that went before (or so it was believed at the time), Led Zeppelin wouldn't have noticed. Their eleventh US tour was also their first in two years and their first since Plant's horrendous car crash. They *could* have played hour-long sets of their shorter songs, in keeping with the punk live shows of the times. Instead, however, Led Zeppelin continued to stretch themselves out over three hours a night. Things weren't what they used to be, however, and the shows had something of a new intensity to them, perhaps borne of the feeling that Led Zeppelin's empire was beginning to show signs of falling, and had been since 1976. Page had to cancel a show mid-way through, thanks to stomach cramps, while another saw him come on stage dressed as a Nazi.

June: RIOT IN TAMPA

No strangers to riots at their shows, Led Zeppelin had to walk off stage at Tampa Stadium on 3 June, for fear of electrocuting themselves. A storm had broken out and rain started to pour into the open-air stadium, so Peter Grant cancelled the show. He intended to bring the band back the following day, but the riot that ensued from the cancellation was so bad that police had to use tear gas to calm the 70,000-strong crowd and the group was banned from returning to the stadium.

July: INCIDENT IN OAKLAND

Despite the slight dip in fortunes for the band, Led Zeppelin's entourage hadn't left their gangster-like behaviour behind. After Peter Grant's son, Warren, was shoved by a security guard backstage at a show in Oakland-Alameda County Coliseum on 23 July, Bonzo gave the security guard a few kicks. When Peter Grant heard about the incident, he and John Bindon, a tough-guy actor and head of security for the tour, took the security guard into a trailer while Richard Cole waited outside. While nobody apart from those that were there saw what happened inside, the trailer ended up covered in blood and the guard came out looking as though he had received a brutal beating. While trying to leave Oakland after the second night's show, Bonham, Grant, Bindon and Cole were arrested, and Bindon subsequently dropped from the Led Zeppelin entourage.

July: KARAC'S DEATH

Almost two years after the car accident, tragedy struck Robert Plant and his family once again when his son Karac died while Plant was still on tour in the US. Aged just six, Karac had been attacked by a respiratory virus on 26 July and died the following day when his condition worsened. Karac's death would inspire 'All My Love', which featured on Led Zeppelin's last studio album, 1979's *In Through The Out Door*. Understandably drained and weary, rumour has it that Plant blamed Page's occult dabblings for the bad luck visited upon him and his family.

October: DAMAGE LIMITATION INTERVIEWS

Not known for giving too many interviews, Jimmy Page certainly
felt spurred on to do so as 1977 drew to a close. 1978 would
be an exceedingly quiet year for the group, but Page had to set it
up: by denying rumours that the band were splitting; explaining
away (in vain) the idea that Led Zeppelin was a cursed band ('I
don't see how the band would merit a karmic attack. All I or we
have attempted to do is go out and really have a good time and
please people'); and try to keep the focus on the music by telling
journalists that he was going through hours of live tapes from
Led Zeppelin's entire career, looking for material to use for a live
album that would better serve the band's legacy.

1979

Early 1979: DOWN TIME

After a quiet 1978, the first half of 1979 didn't see much action
for the group. Maureen Plant had borne Robert another son,
Logan Romero, in January and, perhaps as a way of indulging in
his love for singing without the stress of the band, Plant had
begun sitting in and singing with a West Midlands band known
as Melvin's Marauders. Page, meanwhile, was up in Scotland
at Boleskine House, supporting environmental campaigns to stop
damage to Loch Ness. Since 1978, the most action that Swan
Song had seen came from Dave Edmunds and Maggie
Bell (right).

July: COMEBACK REHEARSALS

With a few songs from their forthcoming live album included, most notably 'In The Evening', Led Zeppelin played two nights in Copenhagen's Falkoner Theatre, on 23 and 24 July – their first live shows in two years. Other than the new songs, the set remained much the same as it had been in 1977, as the band took the chance to flex their live muscles on a much lower scale than their upcoming Knebworth homecoming shows would provide.

August: HEADLINE AT KNEBWORTH

For their first UK shows in four years, Led Zeppelin were understandably nervous. The two nights combined, 4 and 11 August, would see roughly 200,000 people gather to watch the band, supported by the likes of Chas & Dave, Fairport Convention and Todd Rundgren. On the first show, they needn't have worried. The crowd were rabid for their rock gods to return home, and the band provided them with a rock show to judge all other shows by. On the 11th, however, the familiar bad luck struck again when it rained on the outdoor stage and Page's theramin broke down. Never looking to let the band enjoy a good thing for too long, the press slated the show for being the sort of dated, progressive-rock experience that should have gone out two years ago.

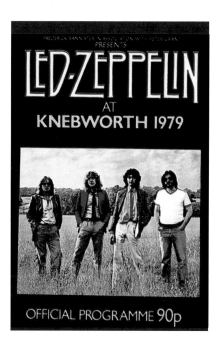

August: IN THROUGH THE OUT DOOR

Named, some say, after the troubles the band found trying to get taken seriously while punk, disco and the UK's burgeoning new-wave scene were rising in popularity (the joke was that it was easier to get popular, or 'In', through the door marked 'Exit'), *In Through The Out Door* (No. 1 UK, No. 1 US) would be Led Zeppelin's final studio album. Slightly delayed upon its release, the wait was worth it for those disappointed by *Presence*. It sounded as though the band had regained a sense of purpose, though this could be because the sessions were mostly led by John Paul Jones and Robert Plant, while Bonham and Page were out chasing their demons. The bassist and singer recorded the bones of the songs during the day, with the other half waiting until the night time to add their parts. Though there's the usual Led Zeppelin rock of 'In The Evening', the group added a synthy groove to the album that gave it more of an unifying feel than *Presence* had, and helped it stand apart in the late-1970s musical landscape.

August: 'ALL MY LOVE'

Page has claimed that he and John Bonham found 'All My Love' to be a little soft for Led Zeppelin. It's true that it stands out as one of the most low-key songs in the group's canon, with Bonham and Page themselves displaying an uncharacteristic restraint in their playing, but the fact that Plant wrote it for his son Karac ('He is a feather in the wind') deserves some respect. Plant and Jones wrote the song together (receiving the sole credit for the track) and, despite the fact that it was never a single, many of the non-rock radio stations in the US picked up on it for airplay alongside some of the soft-rocking artists of the late 1970s.

December: 'FOOL IN THE RAIN'

The last charting Led Zeppelin single in the US, 'Fool In The Rain' (No. 21 US) is also their only song to have an officially released Spanish-language cover version. Page's lyrics for the song were nothing new, being concerned with a woman who his protagonist was meant to meet, but never did. Notably, though, the song has a Latin feel to it which was apparently influenced by Page watching the 1978 World Cup tournament, which was being held in Argentina that year.

1980

April: RICHARD COLE FIRED

When a member of a band's closest entourage is fired, it's a sure sign of a group in distress. Since heroin had entered the group's circle, Cole for one had become an addicted user and, by 1980, Peter Grant felt that he was too debilitated to be able to do his job properly. Grant fired Cole shortly before Led Zeppelin's 1980 European tour. Cole flew to Italy to try to kick his habit and was arrested in Rome when police found what they claimed to be cocaine, among other things, in Cole's hotel room. He was sent to a maximum-security prison for six months.

June-July: EUROPEAN TOUR

Trying to get back to their roots, Led Zeppelin's European tour
saw no laser-light show or large screens. Instead, it was just the
four band members plus equipment, just like in the early days.
Not that they didn't look worse for wear. Page for one had lost a
lot of weight since their last tour in 1977, while Bonham had a
bearded, haggard look not unlike the hermit on the sleeve of *Led
Zeppelin IV*. Without Cole on tour with them the scenes of
wanton destruction had all but disappeared, as the band instead
tried to complete a tour without cancelling dates or having bad
luck befall them.

June: JOHN BONHAM COLLAPSES

Never had there been a man more affected by tour fatigue. Unable to control or curb his drinking, John Bonham just continued apace while he was away from his family, as if he still had the youthful energy that he did when Led Zeppelin first went to America over 10 years before. The cracks in Bonham's health were beginning to show, however, and at the Messezentrum Halle, Nuremburg, Germany, on 27 June, Bonham collapsed only three songs into the set. Despite the official explanation of exhaustion and, later, overeating, the warning signs were there.

July: FINAL LIVE PERFORMANCE

The 1980 European tour was yet another late-period Led Zeppelin tour to be cancelled. Though Bonham would tell the press that everyone had been 'dead chuffed' with the tour, Page cancelled their upcoming dates in France. Led Zeppelin's 7 July show at Eissporthalle, Berlin, would be their last ever as the original four-piece group.

September: JOHN BONHAM DIES

Increasingly despondent over having to leave his family behind while he went on tour, John Bonham must have approached the rehearsals for an upcoming US tour with some trepidation. While being driven to Bray Studios in Berkshire, Bonham asked to stop off at a pub for breakfast, where he downed four quadruple vodkas and orange juice on top of eating some ham rolls. At the rehearsal studio, Bonham continued to drink until, for the first time in his career, he was too drunk to play. The rehearsals were called to a halt and the band retired to Jimmy Page's home, where Bonham continued to drink until he passed out and was put to bed. The following morning the band's tour manager, Benji LeFevre, found John Bonham's dead body in the bedroom. He had died overnight, on 25 September, aged just 32. The official cause of death was asphyxiation caused by choking on his own vomit.

Jimmy Page

Robert Plant

John Bonham

LED ZEPPELIN

John Paul Jones

December: LED ZEPPELIN BREAK UP

Right after Bonham's death, the Led Zeppelin band members and management disappeared into their own worlds, emerging only for Bonham's funeral service on 10 October. Despite rumours that drummers such as Cozy Powell or Carl Palmer may have been considered as Bonham's replacement, no one could *really* replace John Bonham, much less even try to match him. On 4 December Led Zeppelin announced their official break-up, with a press release reading: 'The loss of our dear friend, and the deep sense of harmony felt by ourselves and our manager, have led us to decide that we could not continue as we were.'

THE POST-LED ZEPPELIN YEARS: 1981-2007

1981-2007

With John Bonham gone the three remaining members of Led Zeppelin retreated into their own worlds. Ever the quiet one, John Paul Jones went back to working behind the scenes, mostly recording soundtracks or producing for other artists, before releasing his first solo album in 1999.

Jimmy Page turned up intermittently, mostly as part of a collaborative effort, even getting back in the studio with Robert Plant on a few occasions. Plant himself would see perhaps the biggest post-Led Zeppelin success, carving out an ever-changing, ever-more impressive solo career.

Led Zeppelin's light never dimmed, though. Whether through the high-profile 1990s reggae tribute act, Dread Zeppelin, the entire 1980s heavy metal genre, or Jimmy Page's guitar sound being mimicked the world over, their influence can be felt everywhere. The three remaining members would get together to remind everyone of this on occasion too, most notably at 1985's Live Aid event.

Never beaten, the remaining Led Zeppelin members have done little to tarnish their old band's legacy, while remaining dignified elder statesmen of rock today. As their induction into the UK Music Hall Of Fame showed in 2006, even now people are still looking to them for inspiration. Their 2007 reunion concert saw them work the old magic and further enhance their legendary status.

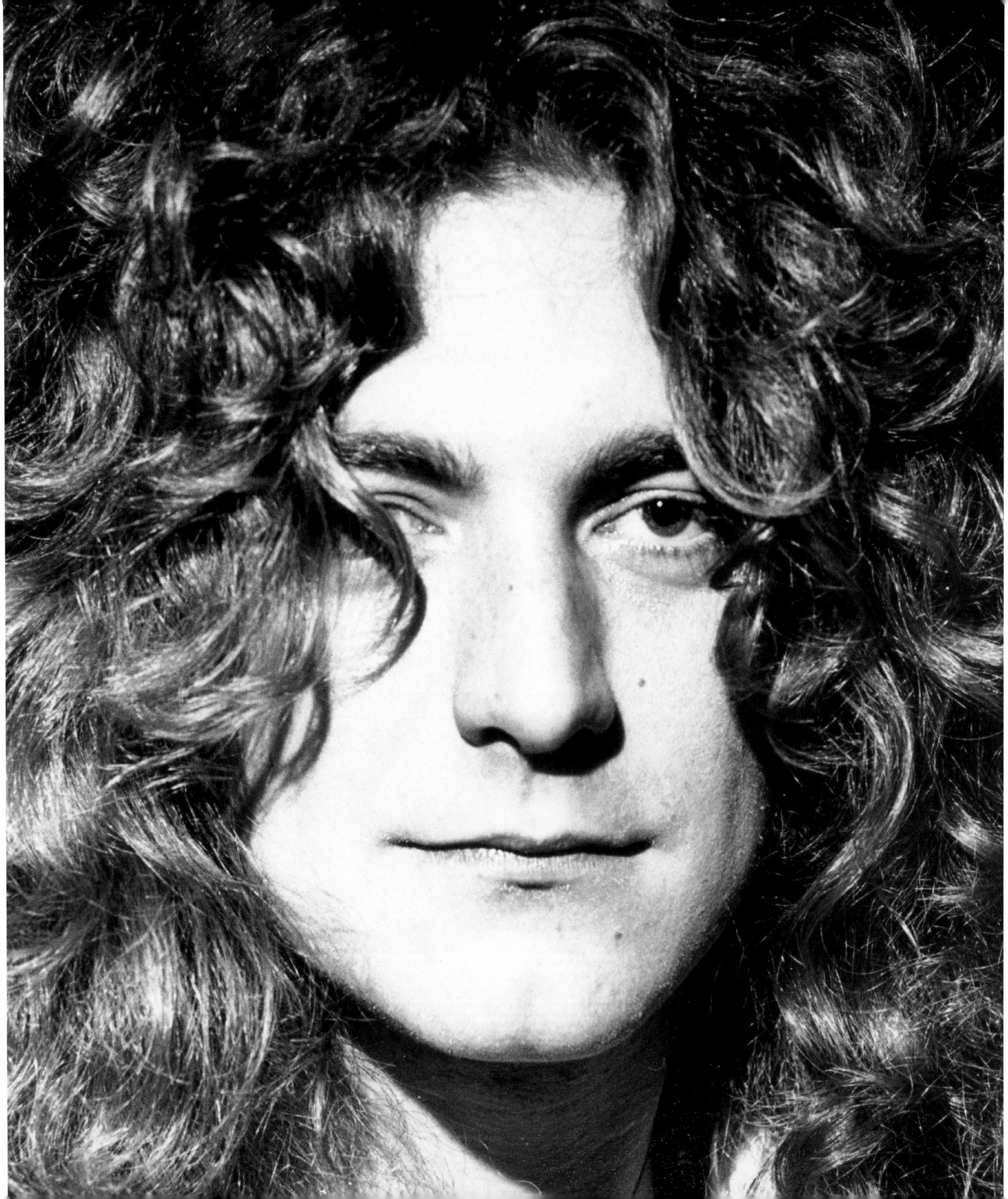

1981

April: THE HONEYDRIPPERS

Never one to be kept away from his passion for long, in the months following John Bonham's death Robert Plant found himself playing 1950s rock'n'roll and R&B on the Northern club circuit with covers band The Honeydrippers. This stint as an anonymous (to the audience, that is) singer gave Plant the chance to return to his roots outside of the Led Zeppelin experience. Perhaps it even taught him to realize he didn't need the group to survive, giving him the opportunity to lay the groundwork for his own solo career.

1982

February: DEATH WISH 2

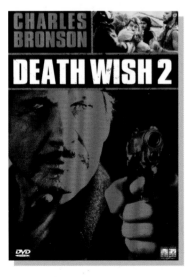

The first sign of life from Jimmy Page since Led Zeppelin announced their split was his soundtrack for Michael Winner's (right) *Death Wish* sequel, *Death Wish 2*. The most interesting thing about this silver-screen tale of one man's revenge was Page's atmospheric soundtrack that heightened the tension of the more violent, suspense-filled parts of the film. He released the soundtrack album on Swan Song the same year.

June: ROBERT PLANT'S PICTURES AT ELEVEN

Even without Led Zeppelin behind him the muse hadn't left Robert Plant, who marked out his solo career in June 1982 with the release of *Pictures At Eleven* on Swan Song. Plant was perhaps as relieved and surprised as anybody when it didn't flop. Largely written with the help of guitarist Robbie Blunt, and featuring Phil Collins on some of the tracks, Plant's first solo album was an eclectic one, happily seeing him view rock'n'roll from new angles, without losing his style or relying on his Led Zeppelin past.

November: CODA

With its low-key release, *Coda* (No. 4 UK, No. 6 US) spelled the end – for a time – of any forthcoming 'new' Led Zeppelin material. A collection of eight outtakes, stretching from 1970 to 1978, it's a sad fact that perhaps they may have been best left unreleased. While featuring nothing particularly awful, there was nothing incendiary about the work that had previously been left on the cutting-room floor. In putting the album together, Page added electronic sound effects to the solo Bonham showcase, 'Bonzo's Montreux', but it wasn't as fitting an end statement as the drummer's earlier 'Moby Dick' showcase had been.

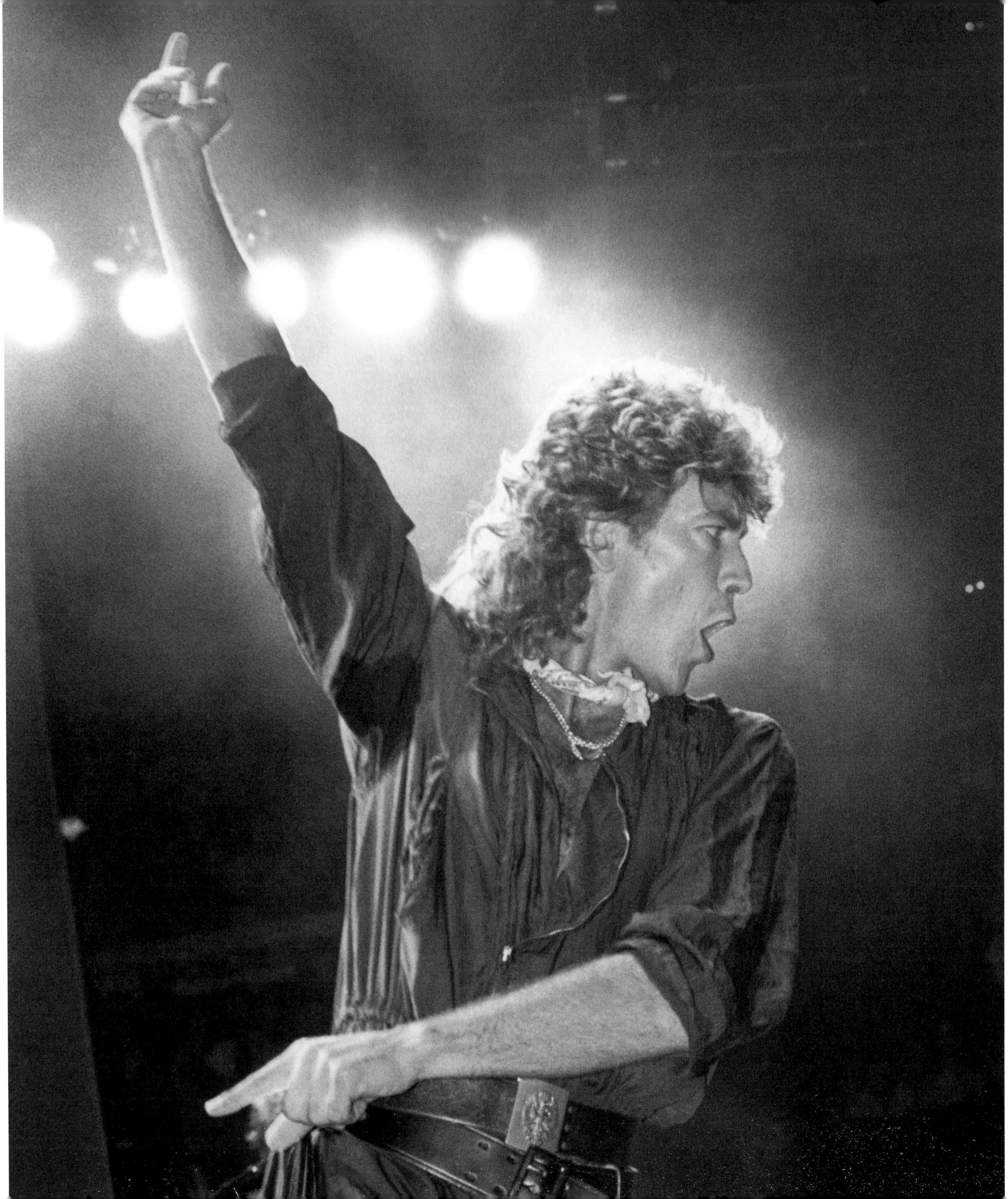

1983

July: PLANT'S THE PRINCIPLE OF MOMENTS

robert plant
the principle of moments

Following on from *Pictures At Eleven*'s success, Plant's second solo album continued down a similar eclectic rock path. Plant refined its predecessor's style by retaining the strongest elements of *Pictures*, but giving them a slightly more commercial bent (the single, 'Big Log', was a Top 20 hit on both sides of the Atlantic). Phil Collins would again drum for Plant and tour with him for the album, seeing Plant quickly proving that his solo success was no flash in the pan. This time Plant released his new album on his own Atlantic subsidiary, Es Paranza.

September: ARMS BENEFIT SHOW

On 20 September 1983 Jimmy Page made only his second public appearance since John Bonham's death (the first was in May 1982, when he and Robert Plant joined Foreigner on stage for an encore). Playing at the ARMS (Action Research For Multiple Sclerosis) Benefit at the Royal Albert Hall, Page was one of the many musicians, including Eric Clapton, Jeff Beck and The Rolling Stones' Charlie Watts, who staged a benefit concert for The Small Faces' bass player Ronnie Lane, who suffered from the disease. The benefit was so successful in the UK that the musicians took the ARMS USA Tour across Dallas, San Francisco, Los Angeles and New York City from 28 November until 9 December.

1984

November: THE FIRM

Long associated with Paul Rodgers (lead singer with Swan Song signing Bad Company), Jimmy Page bounced back from a recent drug-possession arrest by announcing that his first band venture since Led Zeppelin's split would be The Firm with singer Paul Rodgers. Page and Rodgers had first collaborated on the ARMS tour the previous year, giving them a taste for further working together. The two were joined by bassist Tony Franklin and Uriah Heep drummer Chris Slade.

November: THE HONEYDRIPPERS: VOLUME ONE

A supergroup of sorts, The Honeydrippers saw Page and Plant back in the studio together for the first time since their last Led Zeppelin recording sessions. Significantly, the group also saw Page and Jeff Beck playing together for the first time since they sparred in The Yardbirds. With the legendary Nile Rodgers of Chic (left) producing, along with Page and Plant, *The Honeydrippers: Volume One* was a five-track EP of standards covers culled from the studio sessions.

1985

February: THE FIRM'S THE FIRM

A less risky venture than Robert Plant's two previous solo outings, The Firm's *The Firm* saw Jimmy Page and Paul Rodgers head down a more conventional blues-rock path, though it was largely ignored by the critics and only fared a little better in the record-buying public's eye. In retrospect, it was one of Page's best efforts of the 1980s, but as its epic closer, 'Midnight Moonlight', was based on a *Physical Graffiti*-era Led Zeppelin offcut, 'Swan Song', many believed that Page had run out of ideas. The Firm toured in support of the album, but Page and Rodgers refused to play any of their previous bands' work.

May: PLANT'S SHAKEN'N'STIRRED

For his third solo release Robert Plant continued down the inventive rock path that he had been following since *Pictures Of Eleven*. More searching and diverse than the work his former band mate had been following with The Firm, *Shaken'n'Stirred* was this time slightly marred by getting caught up in its own attempts to be inventive, with some listeners finding it a bit too dense to be approached with ease.

July: LIVE AID

The live reunion of the remaining Led Zeppelin members apparently came about when Page and Plant called John Paul Jones to tell him they were going to play the US portion of Bob Geldof's Live Aid benefit concert for famine relief in Ethiopia, and that they were thinking of playing a Led Zeppelin song. Jones is said to have replied, 'I know a Led Zeppelin bass player,' and thus the reunion was on. With Phil Collins and Chic drummer Tony Thompson filling in for John Bonham, the remaining three members of Led Zeppelin played 'Rock'n'Roll', 'Whole Lotta Love' and 'Stairway To Heaven' to an ecstatic crowd. Sadly, when the 20th anniversary *Live Aid* DVD was released, the band members decided that their performance was below par, and refused to let it be included.

1986

April: THE FIRM'S MEAN BUSINESS

Despite the muted reaction to *The Firm*, Page and Rodgers repeated the same blues-rock formula on their second outing, *Mean Business*. Critical reaction was even worse this time and, if the sales were anything to judge by, hardly anyone was listening. Within months of the record's release, Page and Rodgers quietly disbanded the group.

1988

February: PLANT'S NOW & ZEN

For his most-direct rock album since his solo career began, Plant openly acknowledged his Led Zeppelin past. Jimmy Page appeared on two *Now & Zen* tracks, 'Heaven Knows' and 'Tall Cool One', and was credited by the 'ZoSo' symbol. Elsewhere, Plant sampled elements from Led Zeppelin's 'Whole Lotta Love', 'The Ocean', 'Black Dog' and 'Custard Pie' for 'Tall Cool One', on which he also sings snatches of lyrics from 'When The Levee Breaks'. For many Plant's most consistent-sounding release, *Now & Zen* saw him willingly returning to standard rock arrangements for the first time since he had decided to go solo.

May: ATLANTIC RECORDS' 40TH ANNIVERSARY CONCERT

Following the enjoyable reunion for Live Aid, Jimmy Page, Robert Plant and John Paul Jones reunited for Atlantic Records' 40th anniversary concert in Madison Square Garden. The performance was televised to 60 countries across the world, but the reunion would be most notable for John Bonham's son, Jason Bonham, who took the place of his father this time. John Paul Jones would later remark, 'It was uncanny. Jason had every nuance of his father's approach to the group's music. It was as though we'd played together for years.'

1989

June: PAGE'S OUTRIDER

Page must have heard something in Jason Bonham, as he enlisted him to drum on his first (and only – so far) solo album *Outrider*. Returning the favour for that year's *Now & Zen*, Robert Plant also contributed guest vocals to the track 'The Only One'. Unlike Plant, however, Page seemed content to sit back on his hard-rock laurels for *Outrider*. Its monochrome sleeve spoke for the standard hard-rock music the album contained.

November: CARMEN PLANT'S 21ST BIRTHDAY PARTY

Robert Plant's own band played at his daughter Carmen Jane Plant's (right) 21st birthday party, which was celebrated at home in Birmingham in November 1989. Page had taken sometimes to joining Plant's band on stage when he toured his forthcoming solo album, *Manic Nirvana*, and Page and Jason Bonham joined the group on this night, playing some blues standards for the party gathering.

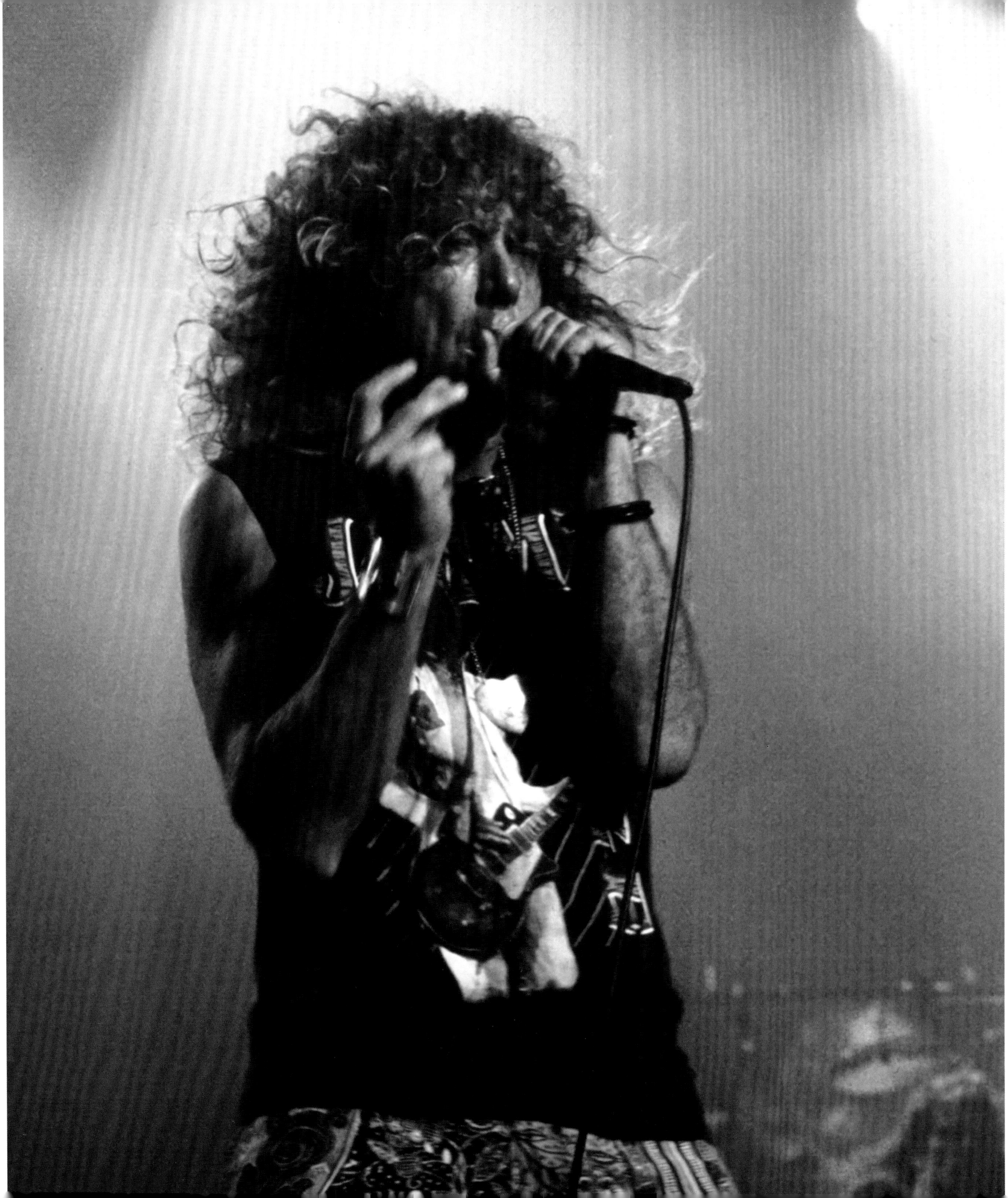

1990

March: PLANT'S MANIC NIRVANA

Picking up from where *Now & Zen* left off, Plant's fifth solo album, *Manic Nirvana*, was an even more stripped-back rocker. Not only had Plant been getting further back to his roots, this time he was losing all of the Led Zeppelin-like frills and flourishes, making this album the most straightforward of his solo releases.

April: JASON BONHAM'S WEDDING

Jason Bonham had been touring with his own band, supporting The Cult and opening their shows each night with a series of Led Zeppelin covers. On 4 April 1990, Jimmy Page, Robert Plant and John Paul Jones attended his wedding celebrations (Bonham Jr. was marrying Jan Charteris) in Stone, Kidderminster, and Jason sat in on a Led Zeppelin set that included 'Custard Pie', 'It'll Be Me', 'Rock & Roll', 'Sick Again' and 'Bring It On Home'.

July: DREAD ZEPPELIN

A Led Zeppelin tribute band of sorts, Dread Zeppelin's debut album, *Un-Led-Ded*, was a selection of Led Zeppelin covers from their first three albums, re-imagined in a reggae style and sung by their front man, Elvis Presley impersonator Tortelvis. The reworking of Led Zeppelin songs with a distinctly different cultural feel predated Page and Plant's own *Unledded* by four years and was given the blessing of Led Zeppelin fans, thanks to its spot-on mixture of humour, inventiveness and reverence for the original music. A number of Dread Zeppelin albums followed in a similar vein, but none had quite the impact of their debut.

September: PROFILED/REMASTERS

Released as a promotional CD to tie in with the release of the *Led Zeppelin* box set the following month, *Profiled* was a collection of Led Zeppelin interviews designed to fill out the band's background in their own words. Among the compilation of various Led Zeppelin-era interview snippets, there were also new interviews from Jimmy Page, Robert Plant and John Paul Jones. The CD was later included in the *Led Zeppelin Remasters* compilation CD released in January 1992.

October: LED ZEPPELIN BOX SET

The notion of a four-CD Led Zeppelin box set seems a little strange for a band unhappy about having singles out under their name, and who viewed each album as an entire body of work on its own. The box set saw Jimmy Page remaster the songs he chose for inclusion, deliberately sequencing them out of sync with any chronological form, so as to bring new perspective to old tunes. The biggest selling points were the inclusion of the solo Page acoustic 'White Summer/Black Mountain Side', the rare 'Immigrant Song' B-side 'Hey Hey What Can I Do', and an unreleased cover of Robert Johnson's 'Travelling Riverside Blues'. A second *Led Zeppelin* box set would be released in March 1993, taking in songs left out from the first set, and adding what was claimed to the be last unreleased rarity, 'Baby Come On Home'.

1993

March: COVERDALE/PAGE

The irony of Jimmy Page teaming up with David Coverdale was that throughout Coverdale's time with Whitesnake in the late 1970s and 1980s, many people noticed his overt similarities to Robert Plant, which led to him being branded David Coverversion in some circles. *Coverdale/Page* would be Page's most successful non-Led Zeppelin related work, though. A collection of co-written originals, it didn't have the range of a Led Zeppelin album, nor was it as drab as Page's solo *Outrider* effort, managing to please hard-rock fans and Page acolytes alike.

May: PLANT'S FATE OF NATIONS

Since Robert Plant's earliest, pre-Led Zeppelin days, he had always had a keen interest in folk music. Though that surfaced, with Plant's input, on Led Zeppelin albums from *III* onwards, *Fate Of Nations* is the first of Plant's solo releases to make his folk influences so

obvious. At times his most personal solo album, Plant's *Fate Of Nations* was yet another corner turned in an increasingly interesting solo career for the singer, and an album that revealed hidden depths over time ('I Believe' addresses Karac Plant's death), while being and his most political ('Network News').

1994

October:
NO QUARTER: JIMMY PAGE & ROBERT PLANT UNLEDDED

Recorded throughout Morocco, Wales and London, the 90-minute MTV *UnLedded* TV show saw Page and Plant, backed by a full orchestra, giving their Led Zeppelin back catalogue the world-music makeover they had been trying to work into the group's sound since their earliest visit to India in 1971. Included were four new Page and Plant originals: 'City Don't Cry', 'Yallah', 'Wonderful One' and 'Wah Wah' (though the latter wouldn't see release until the 2004-anniversary reissue), all with the world influence that characterized the Led Zeppelin covers. Within the confines of what they were attempting, the sister-album release was a success, though John Paul Jones was annoyed that they had called it *No Quarter*, as he was mostly responsible for the Led Zeppelin song by that name, but didn't seem to have been asked to be part of the *UnLedded* project.

1995

January:
INDUCTED INTO ROCK AND ROLL HALL OF FAME

In the same year as Neil Young, Frank Zappa, Al Green, Janis Joplin, Martha Reeves & The Vandellas and The Allman Brothers Band, Led Zeppelin were inducted into the Rock And Roll Hall Of Fame on 12 January 1995. Aerosmith's Joe Perry and Steven Tyler inducted the group, before the remaining members of the band accepted their awards (John Paul Jones dryly thanked his band mates for remembering his number). Later that night, Page, Plant and Jones tore through a handful of Led Zeppelin classics, along with Joe Perry and Steve Tyler, while Young would join the group for a version of 'When The Levee Breaks'.

1997

February: NO QUARTER TOUR

From February until March the following year, Page, Plant and their 40-plus-strong orchestra toured the world in support of *No Quarter*. The tour took in the UK, Europe and the United States in 1995, covering South America, Japan and Australia the following year. Rumours quickly spread that Page and Plant had stopped getting on early into the tour, but nothing came of them. Having sold out in minutes, Page and Plant's continued world-music assault on their back catalogue was greeted rapturously.

August: 'WHOLE LOTTA LOVE'

Not only were Led Zeppelin fiercely opposed to single releases, they were even more opposed to releasing singles in the UK. Apart from the limited 'Trampled Underfoot' single of 1975, 'Stairway To Heaven' and 'D'yer Mak'er' were the only other Led Zeppelin tracks to make it to the vinyl single stage, albeit as promo 7-inches only. It's something of an irony, then, that the first single Atlantic earmarked for release in the US back in 1969 would be the group's first commercial CD single release in the UK. Released in time to bring attention to the band before their *BBC Sessions* was released, this time 'Whole Lotta Love' was edited from 5.36 minutes to 4.50 minutes.

November: BBC SESSIONS

Led Zeppelin's first live release since the *The Song Remains The Same* debacle of 1976, the two-CD *BBC Sessions* set (No. 12 US) was a much better representation of the group's live sound. Heavily bootlegged since their original performances, the otherwise-unreleased versions of Sleepy John Estes' 'The Girl I Love She Got Long Black Wavy Hair' and Eddie Cochran's 'Something Else' were relished by fans when officially released by Led Zeppelin. *BBC Sessions* wasn't without its flaws, however, most notably the editing of the 1971 'Whole Lotta Love' medley and the absence of the 1969-played 'Sunshine Woman', an otherwise-unreleased Led Zeppelin song.

1998

April: PAGE & PLANT'S WALKING INTO CLARKSDALE

Co-produced by 1990s rock-producer extraordinaire Steve Albini (whose work includes production for Pixies, PJ Harvey, Nirvana and The Stooges' March 2007 studio-album comeback), Page & Plant's *Walking Into Clarksdale* wasn't quite the follow-up to *No Quarter* that everybody had hoped for. If *No Quarter* was an understandably cautious collaboration, relying on the tried-and-tested Led Zeppelin material, with only a few new compositions, Page and Plant had to put their money where their mouths were on *Clarksdale*. The brand-new Led Zeppelin rock and force-meets-world compositions were strong, the album just lacked the defining songwriting that characterized the duo's best work. As such, much of it seemed to lack a defining direction, though the single, 'Most High', would win a Grammy for Best Hard Rock Performance in 1999.

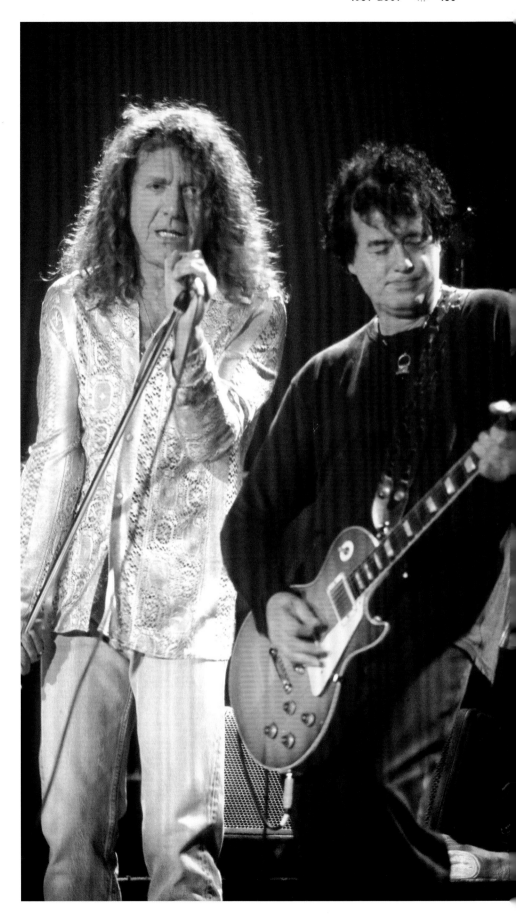

1999

September: JOHN PAUL JONES'S ZOOMA

After years of keeping a low profile with production and soundtrack work, John Paul Jones released his first solo album in September 1999. An instrumental album, it has a range of styles and influences that reveal just how much of an influence Jones had on Led Zeppelin – most notably the later Led Zeppelin albums that branched out from their blues-rock foundation. Solo, Jones worked more like a jazz musician, picking instrumental themes to search and build upon (which included using the London Symphony Orchestra), as opposed to the more immediate, visceral riff-based approach that defined his previous band's music.

2002

July: PLANT'S DREAMLAND

It had been nine years since Robert Plant released a solo album and *Dreamland* sent out mixed signals. Musically, it was a blues-and-folk-based album that carried on from the folk influences of 1993's *Fate Of Nations*. The fact that it was a covers album, however (Plant has two co-author credits), suggested that the old rock god had run out of ideas. Thankfully, listening to it proved otherwise. Galvanized by a new band, The Strange Sensation, Plant was able to revitalize himself by revisiting the sort of songs that had influenced his past (something Bob Dylan himself had done around the same time that Plant was releasing *Fate Of Nations*). With the young Strange Sensation band behind him Plant reconnected with his musical roots in a way unlike he had done before in his solo career. In *Dreamland* he recorded an invigorating album that belied its creator's 54 years of age.

2003

May: LED ZEPPELIN DVD

Just as the same year's *How The West Was Won* would become the audio replacement for *The Song Remains The Same* album release, the 2003 *Led Zeppelin* two-disc DVD set was the definitive document of Led Zeppelin's incredible stage shows. Covering Led Zeppelin's entire touring career from 1969–79, there's plenty of TV appearances and interview footage. The biggest selling points, however, are the entire Royal Albert Hall performance from 9 January 1970, Earls Court footage from 25 May 1975 and footage from Led Zeppelin's first Knebworth homecoming show, 4 August 1979.

October: HOW THE WEST WAS WON

The live album that every Led Zeppelin fan had been waiting for, *How The West Was Won* (No. 5 UK, No. 1 US) presented the best recordings from two concerts recorded in 1972 (25 June, The Forum, and 27 June, Los Angeles and Long Beach Arena) where, arguably, the group were at their live peak. By mixing the best of both shows, the triple-album didn't contain a dud moment. Instead it provided a two-and-a-half-hour document of what Led Zeppelin could do when they were on top form.

2004

November: 'STAIRWAY TO HEAVEN' VOTED NO. 31

Long a ubiquitous part of the world's cultural landscape (a guitar shop in the *Wayne's World* movie banned the song from being played when people were trying out new guitars; the group Butthole Surfers punningly titled their 1988 album *Hairway To Steven*), 'Stairway To Heaven' was voted No. 31 in *Rolling Stone* magazine's November 2004 '500 Greatest Songs Of All Time' cover story. Placed between The Rolling Stones' 'Sympathy For The Devil' (No. 32) and Johnny Cash's 'I Walk The Line' (No. 30). Led Zeppelin's nearest other entry was 'Whole Lotta Love' at No. 75. Though it was a remarkable placing (to be in the top 500 of anything is no mean feat), the fact that 'Stairway' wasn't any higher may have reflected the magazine's current middling opinion of a band it once viewed with derision. Bob Dylan's 'Like A Rolling Stone' topped the chart.

2005

February: GRAMMY LIFETIME ACHIEVEMENT AWARD

The Grammy Lifetime Achievement Award is given out yearly to 'performers who, during their lifetimes, have made creative contributions of outstanding artistic significance to the field of recording'. In 2005, Led Zeppelin were one of those performers. Sadly, John Bonham was no longer alive to see his achievement realized, a fact made even sadder when thinking that he was one of the most outspoken band members against the press's derisory treatment of the group. On the day, Led Zeppelin were one of the 11 artists that year (along with the likes of The Carter Family, Jerry Lee Lewis, Jelly Roll Morton, Janis Joplin and The Staple Singers) that were recognized for their Lifetime Achievement. Some might have said it was actually about three or four lifetimes in one, of course....

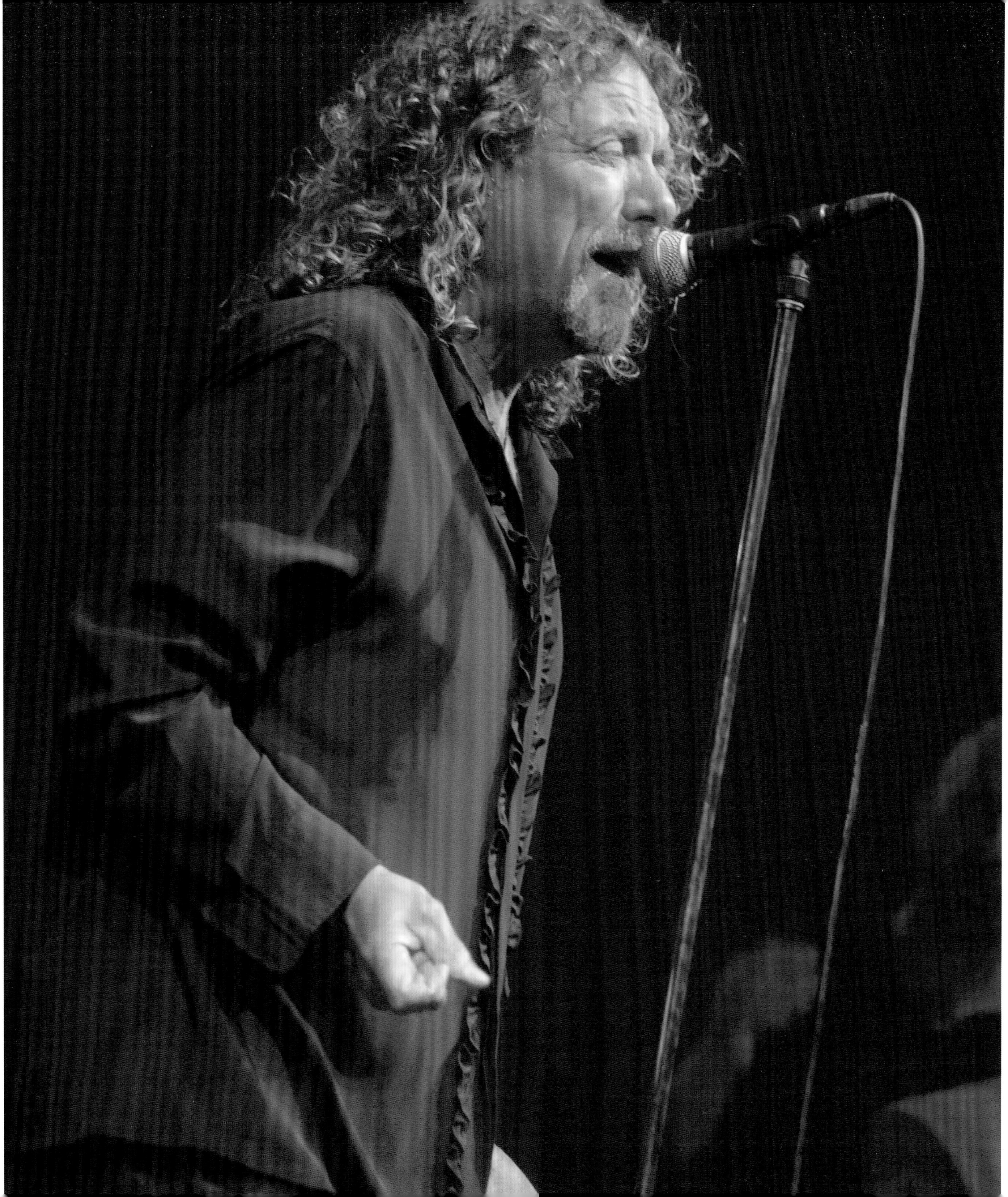

April: PLANT'S MIGHTY REARRANGER

Credited this time to Robert Plant & The Strange Sensation, *Mighty ReArranger* was hailed by many as being Plant's most impressive solo release to date. Easily as varied as the likes of Led Zeppelin's *Houses Of The Holy* or *Physical Graffiti*, *Mighty ReArranger* showed a performer in complete control of all aspects of his musical past: blues, folk, Eastern and world music. While most 'rock dinosaurs' would be happy just to make an album that *rocked* again, Plant was upping the ante for all of his contemporaries by creating an album that resonated with the times, without sounding like a throwback to its creator's own past glories. If Jimmy Page had originally seemed to be the driving genius behind Led Zeppelin's music, *Mighty ReArranger* revealed Plant to be every bit the creative force that his old musical partner was.

November: POLAR MUSIC PRIZE

The Polar Music Prize was founded in 1989 by ABBA manager Stig Anderson and named after Anderson's own Polar Records label. Each year the winners are awarded by the Royal Swedish Academy Of Music and given one million Swedish crowns for their 'exceptional achievements in the creation and advancement of music'. The award is unique in that it doesn't categorize its winners, but treats music of all types as equal, and to be judged on its own terms. Alongside Led Zeppelin, Russian conductor Valery Gergiev was also announced as the winner of the 2006 Polar Music Prize in November 2005.

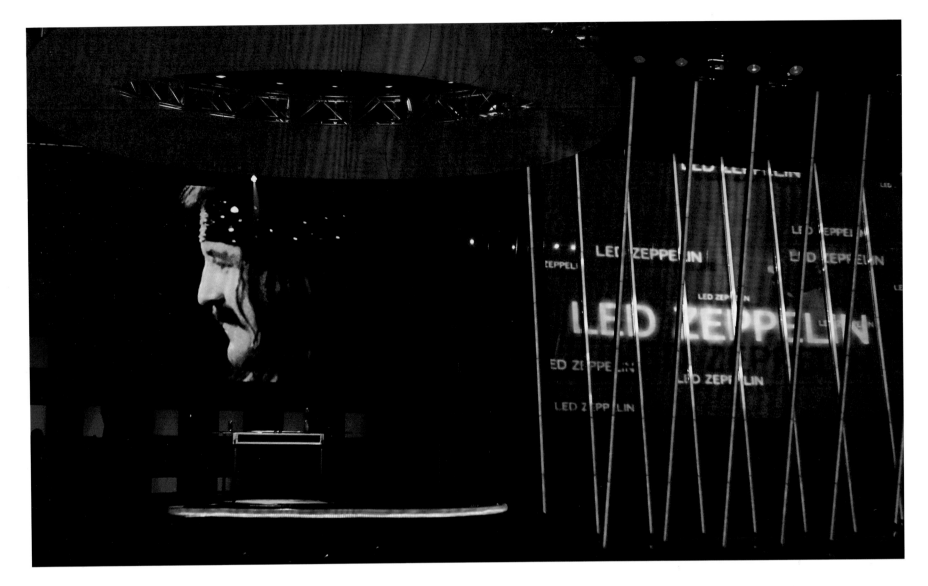

December: PAGE AWARDED OBE

Jimmy Page had often dedicated himself to chartiable causes, such as the ARMS Benefit shows in 1983, or even standing up for environmental causes concerning Loch Ness in Scotland in 1979. Since 1994 he had been an important figure in helping poor children in Rio de Janeiro's shanty towns. With the help of the British charity Task Brasil, Page started the Casa Jimmy safehouse, which provided Rio de Janeiro's underprivileged with clothing, food and job training. In December 2005, aged 61, the one-time occultist was awarded an OBE for his work.

2006

September:
INDUCTED INTO UK MUSIC HALL OF FAME

On 14 November 2006, Led Zeppelin were inducted into the UK Music Hall Of Fame in its third year running. The same year as James Brown, Prince, Brian Wilson, Bon Jovi, Dusty Springfield and Rod Stewart were inducted. Queen's drummer Roger Taylor inducted the group into the Hall Of Fame for their contributions to 'UK music culture'. This gave rise to rumours that the remaining three band members would reform in 2007, but as the official statement was made, it seemed that Jimmy Page, Robert Plant and John Paul Jones were happy pursuing their own separate paths.

2007

December: AHMET ERTEGUN TRIBUTE CONCERT

On 14 December 2006, Atlantic co-founder Ahmet Ertegun died in a coma, two months after falling and hitting his head backstage at a Rolling Stones concert. Led Zeppelin always held Ertegun in high esteem, given everything he had done for the band in their early days. Almost a year later to the day, 10 December 2007, Jimmy Page, Robert Plant and John Paul Jones reunited, with John Bonham's son Jason on drums, to headline a concert held at London's O_2 Arena, in order to raise money for the Ahmet Ertegun Tribute fund. Tickets were allocated through internet ballot, with fans all over the world having to register to be in with a chance of being allotted two tickets priced at £125 each. All the proceeds went to the Ahmet Ertegun charity, and over a million people registered for just 20,000 tickets. Roaring through most of their classics, including 'Whole Lotta Love', 'Stairway To Heaven' and 'Black Dog', the Led Zeppelin concert was not only the reunion of the year, but the rock'n'roll reunion of the decade.

INDEX